HEALTHY LUNCHES IN 10 MINUTES

Glenn Walton

Copyright © 2024 Buddy Jones

All rights reserved

No part of this book may be reproduced, or stored in a retrieval system, or transmitted in any form or by any means, electronic, mechanical, photocopying, recording, or otherwise, without express written permission of the publisher.

Cover design by: M.D. Knight

Printed in the United States of America

CONTENTS

Title Page
Copyright
Importance of Healthy Eating   2
How to Use This Book   4
Essentials for a Quick and Healthy Lunch   6
Essential Kitchen Tools   10
Time-Saving Tips   13
Classic Greek Salad   16
Quick Quinoa Salad   19
Apple Walnut Spinach Salad   22
Mediterranean Chickpea Salad   24
Asian-Inspired Cabbage Salad   27
Caesar Salad with a Twist   30
Berry Spinach Salad   33
Cucumber Dill Salad   35
Avocado Tomato Salad   38
Turkey and Avocado Wrap   40
Hummus and Veggie Sandwich   42
Chicken Salad Lettuce Wraps   44
Tuna Salad Sandwich   47
Egg Salad Wrap   50

Caprese Sandwich	53
Smoked Salmon Bagel Sandwich	55
BBQ Chicken Wrap	58
Falafel Wrap	61
Tomato Basil Soup	64
Quick Veggie Stir-Fry Bowl	67
Lentil Soup	70
Miso Soup	73
Southwest Black Bean Bowl	76
Coconut Curry Soup	79
Spinach and White Bean Soup	82
Chicken and Rice Soup	85
Broccoli Cheddar Soup	88
Zucchini Noodle Bowl	91
Fruit and Nut Mix	94
Yogurt and Berry Parfait	96
Veggie Sticks with Hummus	98
Avocado Toast	100
Cottage Cheese and Fruit	103
Cheese and Whole Grain Crackers	105
Peanut Butter Banana Roll-Up	107
Trail Mix Energy Bites	109
Rice Cake with Nut Butter and Banana	111
Chicken and Hummus Plate	113
Turkey and Cheese Roll-Ups	115
Hard-Boiled Eggs and Veggie Plate	117
Edamame and Quinoa Bowl	119
Shrimp and Avocado Salad	122

Greek Yogurt Chicken Salad	**125**
Beef and Veggie Stir-Fry	**128**
Black Bean and Corn Salad	**131**
Salmon and Asparagus Salad	**134**
Tofu and Veggie Stir-Fry	**137**
Vegan Lentil Salad	**140**
Vegetarian Stuffed Peppers	**143**
Chickpea and Spinach Wrap	**146**
Avocado and Black Bean Salad	**149**
Vegan Buddha Bowl	**151**
Vegetarian Pasta Salad	**154**
Vegan Tacos	**157**
Grilled Veggie Sandwich	**160**
Spicy Peanut Noodles	**163**
Vegan Burrito Bowl	**166**
Quick and Easy Meal Prep	**169**
Encouragement to Stay Healthy	**172**
Thank You	**174**

GLENNWALTON

IMPORTANCE OF HEALTHY EATING

In today's fast-paced world, maintaining a healthy diet can often be a challenge. However, the importance of healthy eating cannot be overstated. A balanced diet provides the nutrients your body needs to function effectively, boosts your immune system, enhances mental clarity, and promotes overall well-being. By choosing healthy foods, you can reduce the risk of chronic diseases such as heart disease, diabetes, and obesity. Additionally, healthy eating habits can improve your energy levels and mood, making you feel more vibrant and ready to tackle your day.

Benefits Of Quick, Nutritious Lunches

While breakfast is often touted as the most important meal of the day, lunch plays a crucial role in keeping your energy levels stable and your mind sharp. Quick, nutritious lunches offer several benefits:

1. **Time Efficiency**: With busy schedules, finding time to prepare a healthy meal can be difficult. Quick lunches save time without compromising on nutrition, allowing you to enjoy a wholesome meal even on your busiest days.

2. **Balanced Nutrition**: By incorporating a variety of food groups, you ensure that your body gets the necessary vitamins, minerals, and macronutrients needed for optimal performance.

3. **Weight Management**: Healthy lunches can help regulate your appetite, preventing overeating later in the day. This balance supports weight management

goals and reduces unhealthy snacking.

4. **Cost-Effective**: Preparing your own lunches at home is often more economical than eating out. You can control portion sizes and ingredients, ensuring quality and saving money.

5. **Enhanced Productivity**: Nutritious lunches fuel your brain and body, leading to better concentration, improved mood, and increased productivity throughout the afternoon.

HOW TO USE THIS BOOK

Welcome to "Healthy Lunches in 10 Minutes," a guide designed to make healthy eating both accessible and enjoyable. This book is structured to provide you with a variety of quick, easy-to-make lunch recipes that fit seamlessly into your busy lifestyle. Here's how to get the most out of this book:

1. **Start with Essentials**: Begin by reading Chapter 1, which covers essential ingredients, kitchen tools, and time-saving tips. This foundation will help you prepare and organize your kitchen for efficient cooking.

2. **Explore by Category**: The recipes are organized into categories such as Salads, Sandwiches and Wraps, Soups and Bowls, Light and Healthy Snacks, Protein-Packed Lunches, and Vegetarian and Vegan Options. Each chapter offers a variety of recipes tailored to different tastes and dietary preferences.

3. **Ingredient Lists and Instructions**: Each recipe includes a list of common household ingredients and easy-to-follow instructions. The goal is to make cooking simple and stress-free, ensuring that you can whip up a delicious meal in just 10 minutes.

4. **Customize and Experiment**: Feel free to customize the recipes to suit your personal preferences or dietary needs. Swap ingredients, adjust seasoning, and make these recipes your own.

5. **Plan Ahead**: Use the Quick and Easy Meal Prep chapter to learn how to plan and prepare ingredients in advance. This will save you even more time and help

you stay consistent with healthy eating.

6. **Stay Inspired**: Keep this book handy in your kitchen and refer to it whenever you need a quick lunch idea. The variety of recipes ensures that you'll never get bored with your meals.

Remember, healthy eating is a journey, and every small step counts. Enjoy the process of creating delicious, nutritious lunches that nourish your body and delight your taste buds.

ESSENTIALS FOR A QUICK AND HEALTHY LUNCH

Must-Have Ingredients

Stocking your kitchen with a selection of versatile, healthy ingredients is key to preparing quick and nutritious lunches. Here are some must-have ingredients to keep on hand:

1. **Fresh Vegetables**
   - **Leafy Greens**: Spinach, kale, arugula, and mixed salad greens.
   - **Cruciferous Vegetables**: Broccoli, cauliflower, and Brussels sprouts.
   - **Root Vegetables**: Carrots, beets, and radishes.
   - **Others**: Bell peppers, cucumbers, tomatoes, avocados, and zucchini.

2. **Fruits**
   - **Berries**: Blueberries, strawberries, raspberries.
   - **Citrus**: Oranges, lemons, limes.
   - **Others**: Apples, bananas, grapes, and avocados.

3. **Proteins**
   - **Animal-Based**: Chicken breast, turkey slices, canned tuna, hard-boiled eggs.
   - **Plant-Based**: Chickpeas, black beans, lentils, tofu, edamame, and hummus.

4. **Whole Grains**
   - **Bread**: Whole grain bread, pita, tortillas.

- **Others**: Quinoa, brown rice, whole grain pasta.

5. **Dairy and Dairy Alternatives**
   - **Cheese**: Feta, mozzarella, cheddar.
   - **Yogurt**: Greek yogurt, plant-based yogurt.
   - **Milk**: Almond milk, soy milk, cow's milk.

6. **Healthy Fats**
   - **Oils**: Extra virgin olive oil, avocado oil.
   - **Nuts and Seeds**: Almonds, walnuts, chia seeds, flaxseeds.
   - **Nut Butters**: Peanut butter, almond butter.

7. **Flavor Enhancers**
   - **Herbs**: Fresh basil, parsley, cilantro, dill.
   - **Spices**: Salt, pepper, paprika, cumin, garlic powder.
   - **Condiments**: Mustard, mayonnaise, soy sauce, balsamic vinegar, apple cider vinegar.

8. **Convenience Items**
   - **Canned Goods**: Canned tomatoes, beans, and tuna.
   - **Frozen Vegetables**: Peas, corn, mixed vegetable blends.
   - **Pre-Cooked Grains**: Ready-to-eat quinoa, rice.

Essential Kitchen Tools

Having the right tools can make meal preparation quick and efficient. Here are some essential kitchen tools for making healthy lunches:

1. **Cutting Board**: A durable, easy-to-clean cutting board.
2. **Sharp Knives**: A chef's knife, paring knife, and

serrated knife.

3. **Mixing Bowls**: Various sizes for preparing and mixing ingredients.
4. **Measuring Cups and Spoons**: For accurate ingredient measurements.
5. **Blender or Food Processor**: For making dressings, smoothies, and chopping ingredients quickly.
6. **Salad Spinner**: To quickly dry leafy greens.
7. **Non-Stick Skillet**: For quick stir-fries and sautéing.
8. **Microwave**: For quick reheating and steaming vegetables.
9. **Storage Containers**: Airtight containers for storing prepped ingredients and leftovers.
10. **Vegetable Peeler**: For peeling fruits and vegetables efficiently.

Time-Saving Tips

To maximize efficiency and make meal preparation a breeze, consider these time-saving tips:

1. **Plan Ahead**: Spend a few minutes each week planning your lunches. Create a menu and shopping list to streamline grocery trips.
2. **Prep Ingredients in Advance**: Wash and chop vegetables, cook grains, and portion out snacks ahead of time. Store them in airtight containers for quick access.
3. **Use Pre-Cut and Pre-Washed Items**: Save time by purchasing pre-cut vegetables, pre-washed greens, and canned beans.
4. **Double Up**: Cook extra portions of grains, proteins, and

vegetables for dinner and use the leftovers for lunch the next day.

5. **Batch Cooking**: Prepare large batches of soups, stews, and salads that can be stored and enjoyed throughout the week.

6. **Simplify Recipes**: Opt for recipes with minimal ingredients and steps to reduce prep and cooking time.

7. **Utilize Convenience Foods**: Incorporate healthy convenience foods like pre-cooked grains, canned beans, and frozen vegetables into your meals.

8. **Keep it Simple**: Focus on simple, fresh ingredients that require minimal preparation. A quick salad, wrap, or bowl can be just as satisfying as a more complex meal.

By keeping these essentials in your kitchen and following these time-saving tips, you'll be well-equipped to prepare quick and healthy lunches that fit seamlessly into your busy lifestyle.

ESSENTIAL KITCHEN TOOLS

Having the right tools in your kitchen can make preparing quick and healthy lunches a breeze. Here are some essential kitchen tools that will help you efficiently create delicious and nutritious meals:

Cutting And Chopping Tools

1. **Cutting Board**: A durable, easy-to-clean cutting board is essential for preparing vegetables, fruits, and proteins. Consider having separate boards for raw meats and fresh produce to prevent cross-contamination.
2. **Sharp Knives**: Invest in a good quality chef's knife, paring knife, and serrated knife. Sharp knives make chopping and slicing quicker and safer.
3. **Vegetable Peeler**: A sturdy peeler will make quick work of peeling vegetables and fruits.
4. **Grater and Zester**: For grating cheese, zesting citrus, and shredding vegetables.

Mixing And Measuring Tools

1. **Mixing Bowls**: Various sizes of mixing bowls for preparing and mixing ingredients. Opt for bowls with non-slip bases for added stability.
2. **Measuring Cups and Spoons**: Accurate measurements are key to consistent results. Keep a set of measuring cups for dry ingredients and a set of measuring spoons

for both dry and liquid ingredients.

Cooking Tools

1. **Non-Stick Skillet**: A non-stick skillet is perfect for quick stir-fries, sautéing vegetables, and cooking eggs. Look for one with a comfortable handle and even heat distribution.
2. **Saucepan**: A medium-sized saucepan for making soups, reheating leftovers, and cooking grains.
3. **Salad Spinner**: To quickly dry leafy greens, ensuring they stay crisp and fresh.
4. **Blender or Food Processor**: Essential for making smoothies, dressings, sauces, and chopping ingredients quickly.
5. **Microwave**: A microwave can be a great time-saver for reheating meals, steaming vegetables, and even cooking some recipes.
6. **Toaster or Toaster Oven**: For toasting bread, bagels, and heating small portions of food.

Storage And Serving Tools

1. **Storage Containers**: Airtight containers in various sizes for storing prepped ingredients, leftovers, and lunch portions. Look for containers that are microwave-safe and stackable to save space.
2. **Lunch Boxes and Bags**: Insulated lunch boxes and bags to keep your meals fresh and portable.
3. **Reusable Snack Bags**: Eco-friendly alternatives to plastic bags for storing snacks and small portions.

Time-Saving Gadgets

1. **Instant Pot or Pressure Cooker**: For quickly cooking grains, beans, and even complete meals with minimal effort.
2. **Electric Kettle**: Boils water quickly for making tea, instant oatmeal, and other quick recipes.
3. **Mandoline Slicer**: For quickly and evenly slicing vegetables.

Miscellaneous Tools

1. **Whisk**: For mixing dressings, sauces, and eggs.
2. **Tongs**: For handling hot foods and serving salads.
3. **Spatula**: A versatile tool for flipping, mixing, and serving food.
4. **Colander**: For draining pasta, rinsing vegetables, and beans.

By equipping your kitchen with these essential tools, you'll be able to streamline your meal preparation process and enjoy the convenience of making quick, healthy lunches. These tools will not only save you time but also make your cooking experience more enjoyable and efficient.

TIME-SAVING TIPS

Preparing quick and healthy lunches doesn't have to be a daunting task. With a few strategic approaches, you can streamline your meal prep and make the most out of your time in the kitchen. Here are some valuable time-saving tips:

Plan Ahead

1. **Weekly Meal Planning**: Spend a few minutes each week planning your lunches. Create a menu and a shopping list based on the recipes you want to make. This will save you time at the grocery store and ensure you have all the ingredients you need.
2. **Batch Cooking**: Cook larger quantities of grains, proteins, and vegetables that can be used in multiple meals throughout the week. Store them in separate containers for easy assembly.

Prep Ingredients In Advance

1. **Chop and Store Vegetables**: Wash, chop, and store vegetables in airtight containers as soon as you get home from the grocery store. This makes it easy to grab and use them when needed.
2. **Pre-Cook Proteins**: Cook and portion out proteins such as chicken, beef, or tofu ahead of time. Store them in the refrigerator or freezer for quick addition to salads, wraps, and bowls.
3. **Make Dressings and Sauces**: Prepare homemade

dressings and sauces in advance and store them in the fridge. This adds flavor to your meals without extra prep time.

Use Convenience Items

1. **Pre-Washed Greens**: Buy pre-washed and bagged salad greens to save time on washing and drying.
2. **Frozen Vegetables**: Keep a variety of frozen vegetables on hand. They are just as nutritious as fresh ones and require no prep time.
3. **Canned Beans and Legumes**: Stock up on canned beans and legumes for quick protein additions to salads and bowls.

Simplify Recipes

1. **Minimal Ingredients**: Choose recipes that require few ingredients and minimal preparation. Simple recipes can be just as delicious and nutritious.
2. **One-Pot or One-Bowl Meals**: Opt for meals that can be made in a single pot or bowl to save on cleanup time.

Efficient Cooking Techniques

1. **Microwave Cooking**: Use the microwave for quick steaming of vegetables, reheating leftovers, and even cooking some grains.
2. **Sheet Pan Meals**: Cook an entire meal on a single sheet pan in the oven. This method is quick, requires minimal cleanup, and is perfect for roasting vegetables and proteins together.

Organize Your Kitchen

1. **Keep Essentials Handy**: Arrange your kitchen so that frequently used items are easily accessible. Keep knives, cutting boards, and mixing bowls within reach.
2. **Label and Organize Containers**: Label storage containers with dates and contents to keep track of prepped ingredients and leftovers.

Utilize Time-Saving Gadgets

1. **Food Processor**: Use a food processor to quickly chop vegetables, make dressings, and mix ingredients.
2. **Instant Pot or Pressure Cooker**: These appliances can cook grains, beans, and proteins in a fraction of the time compared to traditional methods.

Quick Assembly Tips

1. **Mix and Match**: Create a variety of meals by mixing and matching prepped ingredients. For example, combine different proteins, vegetables, and grains to create new and exciting dishes.
2. **Portable Lunches**: Prepare lunches that are easy to pack and take on the go. Mason jar salads, wraps, and bento boxes are great options for portable meals.

By incorporating these time-saving tips into your routine, you'll find that preparing quick and healthy lunches becomes an effortless part of your day. With a little planning and organization, you can enjoy delicious, nutritious meals without spending hours in the kitchen.

CLASSIC GREEK SALAD

Ingredients

- 1 cucumber, diced
- 3 tomatoes, chopped
- 1 red onion, thinly sliced
- 1/2 cup Kalamata olives
- 1/2 cup feta cheese, crumbled
- 2 tablespoons extra virgin olive oil
- 1 tablespoon lemon juice
- 1 teaspoon dried oregano
- Salt and pepper to taste

Instructions

1. In a large bowl, combine the diced cucumber, chopped

tomatoes, and sliced red onion.
2. Add the Kalamata olives and crumbled feta cheese.
3. In a small bowl, whisk together the olive oil, lemon juice, dried oregano, salt, and pepper.
4. Pour the dressing over the salad and toss gently to combine.
5. Serve immediately or refrigerate for up to 2 hours before serving.

Tips & Tricks

- **Make Ahead**: Prepare the vegetables and dressing separately. Combine just before serving to keep the salad fresh.
- **Customize**: Add bell peppers or use cherry tomatoes for a sweeter flavor.
- **Fresh Herbs**: Substitute dried oregano with fresh oregano or mint for a burst of freshness.

Tools Needed

- Cutting board
- Chef's knife
- Mixing bowl
- Small whisk
- Measuring spoons

Fun Fact

Greek salad, or "Horiatiki," is a traditional dish in Greece. It typically doesn't include lettuce and is a staple of the Mediterranean diet, known for its health benefits and fresh, vibrant flavors.

QUICK QUINOA SALAD

Ingredients

- 1 cup cooked quinoa
- 1 cup chickpeas (canned, drained, and rinsed)
- 1 cup cherry tomatoes, halved
- 1 cucumber, diced
- 1/4 cup red onion, finely chopped
- 1/4 cup parsley, chopped
- 3 tablespoons olive oil
- 2 tablespoons lemon juice
- Salt and pepper to taste

Instructions

1. In a large mixing bowl, combine the cooked quinoa,

chickpeas, cherry tomatoes, cucumber, red onion, and parsley.
2. In a small bowl, whisk together the olive oil, lemon juice, salt, and pepper.
3. Pour the dressing over the quinoa mixture and toss to combine.
4. Serve immediately or refrigerate for up to 2 hours before serving.

Tips & Tricks

- **Make Ahead**: Cook the quinoa ahead of time and store it in the refrigerator for up to 3 days.
- **Add-ins**: Feel free to add other vegetables like bell peppers or shredded carrots for extra crunch.
- **Protein Boost**: Add some grilled chicken or tofu for an extra protein punch.

Tools Needed

- Medium saucepan (for cooking quinoa)
- Cutting board
- Chef's knife
- Mixing bowl
- Small whisk
- Measuring cups and spoons

Fun Fact

Quinoa, often called a "superfood," is a complete protein, meaning it contains all nine essential amino acids. It's also gluten-free and rich in fiber, making it a great choice for a healthy diet.

APPLE WALNUT SPINACH SALAD

Ingredients

- 4 cups fresh spinach leaves
- 1 apple, thinly sliced
- 1/4 cup walnuts, chopped
- 1/4 cup feta cheese, crumbled
- 1/4 cup dried cranberries
- 2 tablespoons balsamic vinaigrette

Instructions

1. In a large mixing bowl, combine the spinach leaves, apple slices, chopped walnuts, crumbled feta cheese, and dried cranberries.
2. Drizzle the balsamic vinaigrette over the salad.

3. Toss gently to combine all ingredients.
4. Serve immediately or refrigerate for up to 1 hour before serving.

Tips & Tricks

- **Apple Variety**: Use a crisp apple variety like Granny Smith, Honeycrisp, or Fuji for a nice crunch.
- **Nut Options**: Substitute walnuts with pecans or almonds for a different flavor profile.
- **Extra Sweetness**: Add a drizzle of honey if you prefer a sweeter salad.

Tools Needed

- Cutting board
- Chef's knife
- Mixing bowl
- Salad tongs
- Measuring cups and spoons

Fun Fact

Apples are part of the rose family, just like pears and plums. They have been cultivated for thousands of years and were brought to North America by European settlers in the 17th century.

MEDITERRANEAN CHICKPEA SALAD

Ingredients

- 1 can (15 oz) chickpeas, drained and rinsed
- 1 cup cherry tomatoes, halved
- 1 cucumber, diced
- 1/4 red onion, finely chopped
- 1/4 cup Kalamata olives, pitted and halved
- 1/4 cup feta cheese, crumbled
- 2 tablespoons olive oil
- 1 tablespoon lemon juice
- 1 teaspoon dried oregano
- Salt and pepper to taste

Instructions

1. In a large mixing bowl, combine the chickpeas, cherry tomatoes, cucumber, red onion, and Kalamata olives.
2. Add the crumbled feta cheese to the bowl.
3. In a small bowl, whisk together the olive oil, lemon juice, dried oregano, salt, and pepper.
4. Pour the dressing over the chickpea mixture and toss gently to combine.
5. Serve immediately or refrigerate for up to 2 hours before serving.

Tips & Tricks

- **Make Ahead**: This salad can be made ahead and stored in the refrigerator for up to 3 days. The flavors will meld together, making it even more delicious.
- **Herb Swap**: Substitute dried oregano with fresh herbs like parsley or mint for added freshness.
- **Extra Crunch**: Add some chopped bell peppers or celery for an extra crunch.

Tools Needed

- Cutting board
- Chef's knife
- Mixing bowl
- Small whisk
- Measuring cups and spoons

Fun Fact

Chickpeas, also known as garbanzo beans, are one of the earliest cultivated legumes. They have been grown in the Middle East for thousands of years and are a staple in Mediterranean cuisine.

ASIAN-INSPIRED CABBAGE SALAD

Ingredients

- 2 cups shredded cabbage (green or purple)
- 1 carrot, julienned
- 2 green onions, thinly sliced
- 1/4 cup fresh cilantro, chopped
- 2 tablespoons sesame seeds
- 2 tablespoons soy sauce
- 1 tablespoon rice vinegar
- 1 tablespoon honey
- 1 tablespoon sesame oil
- 1 teaspoon grated fresh ginger

Instructions

1. In a large mixing bowl, combine the shredded cabbage, julienned carrot, sliced green onions, and chopped cilantro.
2. In a small bowl, whisk together the soy sauce, rice vinegar, honey, sesame oil, and grated ginger.
3. Pour the dressing over the cabbage mixture and toss to combine.
4. Sprinkle sesame seeds on top and toss again.
5. Serve immediately or refrigerate for up to 1 hour before serving.

Tips & Tricks

- **Add Protein**: Top the salad with grilled chicken, shrimp, or tofu for a complete meal.
- **Crunch Factor**: Add crushed peanuts or cashews for extra texture.
- **Spice It Up**: Add a dash of Sriracha or red pepper flakes for a spicy kick.

Tools Needed

- Cutting board
- Chef's knife
- Julienne peeler or mandoline slicer
- Mixing bowl
- Small whisk
- Measuring cups and spoons

Fun Fact

Cabbage is a powerhouse of nutrition. It's rich in vitamins C and K, and has been cultivated for over 4,000 years. It is especially popular in Asian cuisine, where it is used in dishes ranging from stir-fries to fermented kimchi.

CAESAR SALAD WITH A TWIST

Ingredients

- 4 cups romaine lettuce, chopped
- 1 cup kale, chopped
- 1/2 cup cherry tomatoes, halved
- 1/4 cup grated Parmesan cheese
- 1/4 cup croutons
- 2 tablespoons Caesar dressing
- 1 tablespoon lemon juice
- 1 teaspoon Dijon mustard
- 1 clove garlic, minced
- Salt and pepper to taste

Instructions

1. In a large mixing bowl, combine the chopped romaine lettuce, chopped kale, and halved cherry tomatoes.
2. In a small bowl, whisk together the Caesar dressing, lemon juice, Dijon mustard, and minced garlic.
3. Pour the dressing over the lettuce mixture and toss to coat evenly.
4. Add the grated Parmesan cheese and croutons to the salad and toss gently.
5. Season with salt and pepper to taste.
6. Serve immediately.

Tips & Tricks

- **Protein Addition**: Add grilled chicken, shrimp, or tofu for a heartier meal.
- **Make It Crunchier**: Use homemade croutons for added freshness and flavor.
- **Healthier Option**: Opt for a low-fat Caesar dressing to reduce calorie intake.

Tools Needed

- Cutting board
- Chef's knife
- Mixing bowl
- Small whisk
- Measuring cups and spoons

Fun Fact

The original Caesar salad was created by Italian-American restaurateur Caesar Cardini in 1924 in Tijuana, Mexico. The salad was prepared tableside for added flair.

BERRY SPINACH SALAD

Ingredients

- 4 cups fresh spinach leaves
- 1 cup strawberries, sliced
- 1/2 cup blueberries
- 1/2 cup raspberries
- 1/4 cup goat cheese, crumbled
- 1/4 cup walnuts, chopped
- 2 tablespoons balsamic vinaigrette

Instructions

1. In a large mixing bowl, combine the fresh spinach leaves, sliced strawberries, blueberries, and raspberries.

2. Sprinkle the crumbled goat cheese and chopped walnuts over the salad.
3. Drizzle with balsamic vinaigrette.
4. Toss gently to combine all ingredients.
5. Serve immediately.

Tips & Tricks

- **Make Ahead**: Prepare the fruit and spinach ahead of time, but add the dressing just before serving to keep the salad fresh.
- **Nut Options**: Substitute walnuts with pecans or almonds for a different flavor profile.
- **Extra Sweetness**: Add a drizzle of honey or maple syrup for a touch of extra sweetness.

Tools Needed

- Cutting board
- Chef's knife
- Mixing bowl
- Measuring cups and spoons

Fun Fact

Berries are not only delicious but also packed with antioxidants, vitamins, and fiber. They are known to help improve brain health and reduce the risk of chronic diseases.

CUCUMBER DILL SALAD

Ingredients

- 2 large cucumbers, thinly sliced
- 1/4 red onion, thinly sliced
- 1/4 cup fresh dill, chopped
- 3 tablespoons Greek yogurt
- 1 tablespoon lemon juice
- 1 tablespoon white vinegar
- 1 teaspoon sugar
- Salt and pepper to taste

Instructions

1. In a large mixing bowl, combine the thinly sliced cucumbers and red onion.

2. In a small bowl, whisk together the Greek yogurt, lemon juice, white vinegar, sugar, salt, and pepper until smooth.
3. Pour the dressing over the cucumber and onion mixture.
4. Add the chopped fresh dill and toss gently to combine.
5. Serve immediately or refrigerate for up to 1 hour before serving.

Tips & Tricks

- **Extra Crunch**: Add some sliced radishes for an extra crunch.
- **Make Ahead**: This salad can be made a few hours in advance and stored in the refrigerator to allow the flavors to meld.
- **Vegan Option**: Use a dairy-free yogurt alternative to make this salad vegan-friendly.

Tools Needed

- Cutting board
- Chef's knife
- Mixing bowl
- Small whisk
- Measuring cups and spoons

Fun Fact

Cucumbers are made up of about 95% water, making them a hydrating and refreshing addition to any meal. They have been cultivated for over 3,000 years and were a favorite in ancient Rome.

AVOCADO TOMATO SALAD

Ingredients

- 2 ripe avocados, diced
- 1 cup cherry tomatoes, halved
- 1/4 red onion, finely chopped
- 1/4 cup fresh cilantro, chopped
- 2 tablespoons lime juice
- 2 tablespoons olive oil
- Salt and pepper to taste

Instructions

1. In a large mixing bowl, combine the diced avocados, halved cherry tomatoes, finely chopped red onion, and chopped cilantro.

2. In a small bowl, whisk together the lime juice, olive oil, salt, and pepper.
3. Pour the dressing over the avocado and tomato mixture and toss gently to combine.
4. Serve immediately or refrigerate for up to 1 hour before serving.

Tips & Tricks

- **Prevent Browning**: To prevent the avocados from browning, add the lime juice immediately after dicing them.
- **Add Protein**: Add grilled chicken or shrimp for a more substantial meal.
- **Herb Variation**: Substitute cilantro with fresh basil or parsley for a different flavor profile.

Tools Needed

- Cutting board
- Chef's knife
- Mixing bowl
- Small whisk
- Measuring cups and spoons

Fun Fact

Avocados are often called "nature's butter" because of their creamy texture. They are rich in healthy monounsaturated fats, which are beneficial for heart health.

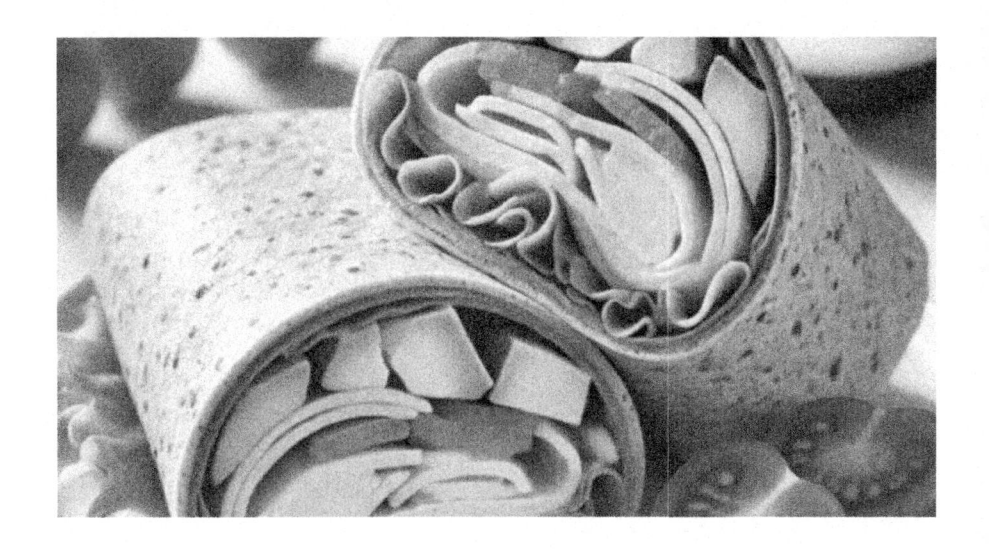

TURKEY AND AVOCADO WRAP

Ingredients

- 1 whole wheat tortilla
- 4 slices of turkey breast
- 1/2 avocado, sliced
- 1/2 cup lettuce leaves
- 1/4 cup cherry tomatoes, halved
- 1 tablespoon mustard (optional)
- Salt and pepper to taste

Instructions

1. Lay the whole wheat tortilla flat on a clean surface.
2. Spread the mustard evenly over the tortilla (if using).
3. Layer the turkey slices, avocado, lettuce, and cherry

tomatoes in the center of the tortilla.
4. Sprinkle with salt and pepper to taste.
5. Fold the sides of the tortilla over the filling, then roll it up tightly from the bottom to the top.
6. Cut the wrap in half and serve immediately.

Tips & Tricks

- **Extra Flavor**: Add a slice of cheese or a handful of sprouts for extra flavor and texture.
- **Make Ahead**: Prepare the wrap the night before and store it in the refrigerator for an easy grab-and-go lunch.
- **Variation**: Substitute the turkey with grilled chicken or smoked salmon for a different twist.

Tools Needed

- Cutting board
- Chef's knife
- Spreading knife

Fun Fact

Avocados are often referred to as "alligator pears" due to their shape and rough skin. They are native to Central and South America and have been cultivated for thousands of years.

HUMMUS AND VEGGIE SANDWICH

Ingredients

- 2 slices whole grain bread
- 1/4 cup hummus
- 1/4 cucumber, thinly sliced
- 1/4 red bell pepper, thinly sliced
- 1 small carrot, grated
- 1/4 cup spinach leaves
- Salt and pepper to taste

Instructions

1. Spread the hummus evenly over one side of each slice of whole grain bread.
2. Layer the cucumber slices, red bell pepper slices, grated

carrot, and spinach leaves on one slice of bread.
3. Sprinkle with salt and pepper to taste.
4. Place the second slice of bread on top, hummus side down, to form a sandwich.
5. Cut the sandwich in half and serve immediately.

Tips & Tricks

- **Flavor Variations**: Add a few slices of avocado or a handful of sprouts for extra flavor and nutrition.
- **Bread Choice**: Use your favorite type of whole grain bread, such as multigrain or sprouted grain, for added texture and nutrients.
- **Make It a Wrap**: Turn this sandwich into a wrap by using a whole wheat tortilla instead of bread.

Tools Needed

- Cutting board
- Chef's knife
- Spreading knife
- Grater

Fun Fact

Hummus, a popular Middle Eastern dip made from chickpeas, tahini, lemon juice, and garlic, has been enjoyed for centuries. It is known for its creamy texture and rich nutritional profile, being high in protein and fiber.

CHICKEN SALAD LETTUCE WRAPS

Ingredients

- 1 cup cooked chicken breast, diced
- 1/4 cup Greek yogurt
- 1 tablespoon mayonnaise
- 1 celery stalk, finely chopped
- 1/4 cup red grapes, halved
- 1 tablespoon fresh parsley, chopped
- 1 tablespoon lemon juice
- Salt and pepper to taste
- 6 large lettuce leaves (such as romaine or butter lettuce)

Instructions

1. In a mixing bowl, combine the diced chicken, Greek yogurt, mayonnaise, chopped celery, halved grapes, chopped parsley, lemon juice, salt, and pepper.
2. Mix until all ingredients are well combined.
3. Spoon the chicken salad mixture into the center of each lettuce leaf.
4. Roll or fold the lettuce leaves around the chicken salad to create wraps.
5. Serve immediately.

Tips & Tricks

- **Make Ahead**: Prepare the chicken salad mixture ahead of time and store it in the refrigerator. Assemble the wraps just before serving.
- **Add Crunch**: Include chopped nuts, such as almonds or walnuts, for added texture.
- **Flavor Boost**: Add a dash of Dijon mustard or a sprinkle of curry powder for extra flavor.

Tools Needed

- Cutting board
- Chef's knife
- Mixing bowl
- Measuring cups and spoons
- Spoon for mixing

Fun Fact

Lettuce wraps are a popular alternative to traditional wraps and sandwiches. They are low in calories and carbs, making them a great option for those looking to reduce their intake while still enjoying a satisfying meal.

TUNA SALAD SANDWICH

Ingredients

- 1 can (5 oz) tuna, drained
- 2 tablespoons Greek yogurt
- 1 tablespoon mayonnaise
- 1 teaspoon Dijon mustard
- 1 celery stalk, finely chopped
- 1 tablespoon red onion, finely chopped
- 1 tablespoon pickle relish
- Salt and pepper to taste
- 4 slices whole grain bread
- Lettuce leaves (optional)
- Tomato slices (optional)

Instructions

1. In a mixing bowl, combine the drained tuna, Greek yogurt, mayonnaise, Dijon mustard, chopped celery, chopped red onion, and pickle relish.
2. Mix until all ingredients are well combined.
3. Season with salt and pepper to taste.
4. Spread the tuna salad evenly over two slices of whole grain bread.
5. Top with lettuce leaves and tomato slices, if desired.
6. Place the remaining slices of bread on top to form sandwiches.
7. Cut the sandwiches in half and serve immediately.

Tips & Tricks

- **Make Ahead**: Prepare the tuna salad mixture ahead of time and store it in the refrigerator for up to 2 days.
- **Add Crunch**: Include chopped nuts, such as almonds or walnuts, for added texture.
- **Flavor Boost**: Add a dash of hot sauce or a sprinkle of fresh herbs like dill or parsley for extra flavor.

Tools Needed

- Cutting board
- Chef's knife
- Mixing bowl
- Measuring cups and spoons

- Spoon for mixing

Fun Fact

Tuna is a great source of lean protein and omega-3 fatty acids, which are beneficial for heart health. It has been a popular ingredient in sandwiches since the early 20th century.

EGG SALAD WRAP

Ingredients

- 4 hard-boiled eggs, chopped
- 2 tablespoons Greek yogurt
- 1 tablespoon mayonnaise
- 1 teaspoon Dijon mustard
- 1 celery stalk, finely chopped
- 1 tablespoon chives, finely chopped
- Salt and pepper to taste
- 2 whole wheat tortillas
- Lettuce leaves (optional)

Instructions

1. In a mixing bowl, combine the chopped hard-

boiled eggs, Greek yogurt, mayonnaise, Dijon mustard, chopped celery, and chives.
2. Mix until all ingredients are well combined.
3. Season with salt and pepper to taste.
4. Lay the whole wheat tortillas flat on a clean surface.
5. Spread the egg salad mixture evenly over the tortillas.
6. Top with lettuce leaves, if desired.
7. Roll the tortillas tightly to form wraps.
8. Cut the wraps in half and serve immediately.

Tips & Tricks

- **Make Ahead**: Prepare the egg salad mixture ahead of time and store it in the refrigerator for up to 2 days.
- **Add Flavor**: Add a dash of hot sauce or a sprinkle of paprika for extra flavor.
- **Variation**: Turn this wrap into a sandwich by using whole grain bread instead of tortillas.

Tools Needed

- Cutting board
- Chef's knife
- Mixing bowl
- Measuring cups and spoons
- Spoon for mixing

Fun Fact

Eggs are one of the most versatile ingredients in the kitchen. They are a great source of high-quality protein and contain essential nutrients such as vitamins B12 and D.

CAPRESE SANDWICH

Ingredients

- 2 slices whole grain bread
- 1 ripe tomato, sliced
- 1/4 cup fresh mozzarella, sliced
- 4-5 fresh basil leaves
- 1 tablespoon balsamic glaze
- 1 tablespoon olive oil
- Salt and pepper to taste

Instructions

1. Drizzle the olive oil over one side of each slice of whole grain bread.
2. Layer the tomato slices, fresh mozzarella slices, and

basil leaves on one slice of bread.
3. Drizzle the balsamic glaze over the toppings.
4. Sprinkle with salt and pepper to taste.
5. Place the second slice of bread on top, olive oil side down, to form a sandwich.
6. Cut the sandwich in half and serve immediately.

Tips & Tricks

- **Grill It**: For a warm and toasty version, grill the sandwich in a panini press or on a stovetop skillet until the bread is golden brown and the cheese is melted.
- **Extra Flavor**: Add a few slices of avocado or a handful of arugula for added flavor and nutrition.
- **Make Ahead**: Prepare the ingredients ahead of time and assemble the sandwich just before serving.

Tools Needed

- Cutting board
- Chef's knife
- Spreading knife

Fun Fact

The Caprese salad, which inspires this sandwich, originated from the island of Capri in Italy. It is traditionally made with fresh tomatoes, mozzarella, basil, olive oil, and a sprinkle of salt.

SMOKED SALMON BAGEL SANDWICH

Ingredients

- 1 whole grain bagel, sliced
- 3 oz smoked salmon
- 2 tablespoons cream cheese
- 1/4 red onion, thinly sliced
- 1/4 cucumber, thinly sliced
- 1 tablespoon capers
- Fresh dill, for garnish
- Lemon wedges, for serving

Instructions

1. Toast the bagel halves until golden brown.

2. Spread the cream cheese evenly on both halves of the toasted bagel.
3. Layer the smoked salmon, thinly sliced red onion, and cucumber on the bottom half of the bagel.
4. Sprinkle capers over the toppings.
5. Garnish with fresh dill.
6. Place the top half of the bagel over the fillings to form a sandwich.
7. Serve immediately with lemon wedges on the side.

Tips & Tricks

- **Variation**: Add a few slices of avocado for extra creaminess and flavor.
- **Herb Swap**: Substitute dill with fresh chives or parsley if you prefer.
- **Make Ahead**: Assemble the sandwich without the cream cheese and store it in the refrigerator. Add the cream cheese just before serving to prevent the bagel from getting soggy.

Tools Needed

- Toaster
- Cutting board
- Chef's knife
- Spreading knife

Fun Fact

Smoked salmon, also known as lox, has been enjoyed for centuries and is particularly popular in Jewish cuisine. It is rich in omega-3 fatty acids, which are beneficial for heart health.

BBQ CHICKEN WRAP

Ingredients

- 1 whole wheat tortilla
- 1 cup cooked chicken breast, shredded
- 2 tablespoons BBQ sauce
- 1/4 cup shredded lettuce
- 1/4 cup shredded cheddar cheese
- 1/4 cup corn kernels (fresh or canned, drained)
- 1/4 red onion, thinly sliced
- Salt and pepper to taste

Instructions

1. In a mixing bowl, combine the shredded chicken and BBQ sauce until the chicken is evenly coated.

2. Lay the whole wheat tortilla flat on a clean surface.
3. Layer the BBQ chicken, shredded lettuce, shredded cheddar cheese, corn kernels, and thinly sliced red onion in the center of the tortilla.
4. Sprinkle with salt and pepper to taste.
5. Fold the sides of the tortilla over the filling, then roll it up tightly from the bottom to the top.
6. Cut the wrap in half and serve immediately.

Tips & Tricks

- **Add Extra Flavor**: Include a few slices of avocado or a handful of chopped cilantro for added flavor and nutrition.
- **Make Ahead**: Prepare the BBQ chicken mixture ahead of time and store it in the refrigerator. Assemble the wrap just before serving.
- **Variation**: Use a different type of cheese, such as pepper jack, for a spicy kick.

Tools Needed

- Cutting board
- Chef's knife
- Mixing bowl
- Measuring cups and spoons

Fun Fact

BBQ sauce has a rich history and varies by region. In the United States, popular types include Kansas City, Texas, Memphis, and

Carolina styles, each with its unique flavor profile and ingredients.

FALAFEL WRAP

Ingredients

- 1 whole wheat tortilla
- 4-5 falafel balls, cooked
- 1/4 cup hummus
- 1/4 cup cucumber, diced
- 1/4 cup tomato, diced
- 1/4 cup red onion, thinly sliced
- 1/4 cup lettuce leaves, chopped
- 2 tablespoons tzatziki sauce (optional)
- Salt and pepper to taste

Instructions

1. Lay the whole wheat tortilla flat on a clean surface.

2. Spread the hummus evenly over the tortilla.
3. Place the falafel balls in the center of the tortilla.
4. Add the diced cucumber, diced tomato, thinly sliced red onion, and chopped lettuce leaves on top of the falafel.
5. Drizzle with tzatziki sauce, if using.
6. Sprinkle with salt and pepper to taste.
7. Fold the sides of the tortilla over the filling, then roll it up tightly from the bottom to the top.
8. Cut the wrap in half and serve immediately.

Tips & Tricks

- **Make Ahead**: Prepare the falafel ahead of time and store it in the refrigerator. Assemble the wrap just before serving.
- **Add Extra Flavor**: Include a few olives or a sprinkle of feta cheese for added flavor.
- **Vegan Option**: Ensure the tzatziki sauce is dairy-free or use a vegan alternative.

Tools Needed

- Cutting board
- Chef's knife
- Mixing bowl
- Measuring cups and spoons

Fun Fact

Falafel is a popular Middle Eastern dish made from ground chickpeas or fava beans. It is often served in pita bread or as part of a mezze platter and is enjoyed worldwide for its delicious flavor and crispy texture.

TOMATO BASIL SOUP

Ingredients

- 2 cans (14.5 oz each) diced tomatoes
- 1 cup vegetable broth
- 1/2 cup onion, finely chopped
- 2 cloves garlic, minced
- 1/4 cup fresh basil leaves, chopped
- 2 tablespoons olive oil
- 1 teaspoon sugar
- Salt and pepper to taste
- Optional: 1/4 cup heavy cream or 1/2 cup milk for a creamier texture

Instructions

1. In a large pot, heat the olive oil over medium heat.
2. Add the chopped onion and cook until softened, about 5 minutes.
3. Add the minced garlic and cook for another 1-2 minutes, until fragrant.
4. Pour in the diced tomatoes (with their juice) and vegetable broth.
5. Stir in the sugar, salt, and pepper.
6. Bring the mixture to a boil, then reduce the heat and let it simmer for 10 minutes.
7. Remove from heat and stir in the chopped fresh basil.
8. For a smoother texture, use an immersion blender to puree the soup until smooth, or carefully transfer the soup in batches to a blender.
9. Optional: Stir in the heavy cream or milk for a creamier soup.
10. Serve hot, garnished with additional basil leaves if desired.

Tips & Tricks

- **Add Spice**: For a bit of heat, add a pinch of red pepper flakes when cooking the onions.
- **Make Ahead**: This soup can be made ahead and stored in the refrigerator for up to 3 days or frozen for up to 3 months.
- **Serve with**: Pair with a grilled cheese sandwich for a classic combo.

Tools Needed

- Large pot
- Cutting board
- Chef's knife
- Immersion blender or regular blender
- Measuring cups and spoons

Fun Fact

Tomato soup has been a comfort food staple for centuries, with the first written recipes dating back to the early 19th century. It's enjoyed worldwide and is often paired with a grilled cheese sandwich in American cuisine.

QUICK VEGGIE STIR-FRY BOWL

Ingredients

- 1 cup broccoli florets
- 1 cup bell pepper, sliced
- 1 cup snap peas
- 1 carrot, julienned
- 2 tablespoons soy sauce
- 1 tablespoon sesame oil
- 1 tablespoon olive oil
- 2 cloves garlic, minced
- 1 teaspoon grated ginger
- 1 cup cooked brown rice
- Sesame seeds, for garnish
- Green onions, sliced, for garnish

Instructions

1. Heat the olive oil and sesame oil in a large skillet or wok over medium-high heat.
2. Add the minced garlic and grated ginger, and sauté for 1-2 minutes until fragrant.
3. Add the broccoli florets, bell pepper slices, snap peas, and julienned carrot to the skillet.
4. Stir-fry the vegetables for 5-7 minutes, until they are tender but still crisp.
5. Pour the soy sauce over the vegetables and stir to coat evenly.
6. Serve the stir-fried vegetables over a bed of cooked brown rice.
7. Garnish with sesame seeds and sliced green onions.
8. Serve immediately.

Tips & Tricks

- **Protein Boost**: Add cooked chicken, tofu, or shrimp for extra protein.
- **Extra Flavor**: Add a dash of hoisin sauce or a sprinkle of red pepper flakes for more flavor.
- **Make Ahead**: Prep the vegetables ahead of time and store them in the refrigerator for a quick meal.

Tools Needed

- Cutting board
- Chef's knife

- Large skillet or wok
- Wooden spoon or spatula
- Measuring cups and spoons

Fun Fact

Stir-frying is a cooking technique that originated in China and has been used for over 2,000 years. It involves cooking ingredients quickly at high heat, which helps to preserve their nutrients and flavors.

LENTIL SOUP

Ingredients

- 1 cup dried lentils, rinsed and drained
- 1 carrot, diced
- 1 celery stalk, diced
- 1 small onion, finely chopped
- 2 cloves garlic, minced
- 4 cups vegetable broth
- 1 can (14.5 oz) diced tomatoes
- 1 teaspoon ground cumin
- 1 teaspoon dried thyme
- 1 bay leaf
- 2 tablespoons olive oil
- Salt and pepper to taste

- Fresh parsley, chopped (for garnish)

Instructions

1. Heat the olive oil in a large pot over medium heat.
2. Add the chopped onion, diced carrot, and diced celery. Sauté for 5-7 minutes, until the vegetables are softened.
3. Add the minced garlic and cook for another 1-2 minutes, until fragrant.
4. Stir in the rinsed lentils, vegetable broth, diced tomatoes (with their juice), ground cumin, dried thyme, and bay leaf.
5. Bring the mixture to a boil, then reduce the heat and let it simmer for 20-25 minutes, until the lentils are tender.
6. Remove the bay leaf and season the soup with salt and pepper to taste.
7. Serve hot, garnished with chopped fresh parsley.

Tips & Tricks

- **Add Greens**: Stir in a handful of spinach or kale during the last 5 minutes of cooking for added nutrition.
- **Make Ahead**: This soup can be made ahead and stored in the refrigerator for up to 3 days or frozen for up to 3 months.
- **Creamy Texture**: For a creamier texture, use an immersion blender to partially blend the soup before serving.

Tools Needed

- Large pot
- Cutting board
- Chef's knife
- Wooden spoon or spatula
- Measuring cups and spoons

Fun Fact

Lentils are one of the oldest cultivated crops, dating back to 8,000 B.C. They are a great source of protein, fiber, and essential nutrients, making them a staple in many diets around the world.

MISO SOUP

Ingredients

- 4 cups water
- 1/4 cup miso paste (white or yellow)
- 1/2 cup tofu, cubed
- 1/4 cup green onions, thinly sliced
- 1/4 cup seaweed (wakame), rehydrated
- 1 tablespoon soy sauce
- 1 teaspoon grated ginger (optional)

Instructions

1. In a medium pot, bring the water to a gentle simmer over medium heat.
2. In a small bowl, mix the miso paste with a few

tablespoons of hot water to dissolve it, then add it to the pot.
3. Add the cubed tofu, rehydrated seaweed, and grated ginger (if using) to the pot.
4. Stir in the soy sauce.
5. Simmer for 5-7 minutes, until the tofu is heated through.
6. Remove from heat and stir in the sliced green onions.
7. Serve hot.

Tips & Tricks

- **Add Flavor**: For extra depth of flavor, add a splash of mirin or a few drops of sesame oil.
- **Customize**: Feel free to add other ingredients such as mushrooms, spinach, or thinly sliced carrots.
- **Quick Rehydration**: Soak the seaweed in warm water for 5 minutes to rehydrate before adding it to the soup.

Tools Needed

- Medium pot
- Small bowl
- Spoon for stirring
- Measuring cups and spoons

Fun Fact

Miso is a traditional Japanese seasoning made by fermenting soybeans with salt and koji (a type of fungus). It has been used in Japanese cuisine for over 1,000 years and is known for its rich

GLENNWALTON

umami flavor.

SOUTHWEST BLACK BEAN BOWL

Ingredients

- 1 can (15 oz) black beans, drained and rinsed
- 1 cup corn kernels (fresh or canned, drained)
- 1 cup cherry tomatoes, halved
- 1/2 red onion, finely chopped
- 1 avocado, diced
- 1/4 cup fresh cilantro, chopped
- 1/4 cup feta cheese, crumbled
- 1 tablespoon lime juice
- 1 tablespoon olive oil
- 1 teaspoon ground cumin
- 1 teaspoon chili powder
- Salt and pepper to taste

Instructions

1. In a large mixing bowl, combine the black beans, corn kernels, halved cherry tomatoes, finely chopped red onion, and diced avocado.
2. In a small bowl, whisk together the lime juice, olive oil, ground cumin, chili powder, salt, and pepper.
3. Pour the dressing over the black bean mixture and toss to coat evenly.
4. Serve the salad in bowls and top with chopped fresh cilantro and crumbled feta cheese.
5. Serve immediately.

Tips & Tricks

- **Protein Boost**: Add grilled chicken or shrimp for extra protein.
- **Spice It Up**: Add a diced jalapeño or a splash of hot sauce for extra heat.
- **Make Ahead**: Prepare the salad ahead of time and store it in the refrigerator for up to 2 days. Add the avocado just before serving to prevent browning.

Tools Needed

- Cutting board
- Chef's knife
- Mixing bowl
- Small whisk
- Measuring cups and spoons

Fun Fact

Black beans are a staple in Latin American cuisine and are known for their high fiber and protein content. They are often used in a variety of dishes, from soups to salads, and are especially popular in Mexican and Caribbean cuisines.

COCONUT CURRY SOUP

Ingredients

- 1 tablespoon olive oil
- 1 onion, finely chopped
- 2 cloves garlic, minced
- 1 tablespoon ginger, grated
- 1 tablespoon red curry paste
- 1 can (14 oz) coconut milk
- 2 cups vegetable broth
- 1 cup sweet potato, diced
- 1 red bell pepper, sliced
- 1 cup baby spinach
- 1 tablespoon lime juice
- Salt and pepper to taste

- Fresh cilantro, chopped (for garnish)

Instructions

1. Heat the olive oil in a large pot over medium heat.
2. Add the chopped onion and sauté until softened, about 5 minutes.
3. Add the minced garlic and grated ginger, and cook for another 1-2 minutes until fragrant.
4. Stir in the red curry paste and cook for 1 minute, stirring constantly.
5. Pour in the coconut milk and vegetable broth, and bring to a simmer.
6. Add the diced sweet potato and sliced red bell pepper. Simmer for 10-15 minutes, until the vegetables are tender.
7. Stir in the baby spinach and cook until wilted, about 2 minutes.
8. Add the lime juice and season with salt and pepper to taste.
9. Serve hot, garnished with chopped fresh cilantro.

Tips & Tricks

- **Protein Addition**: Add cooked chicken, shrimp, or tofu for extra protein.
- **Extra Veggies**: Add other vegetables such as mushrooms, green beans, or carrots for more variety.
- **Make Ahead**: This soup can be made ahead and stored in the refrigerator for up to 3 days or frozen for up to 3 months.

Tools Needed

- Large pot
- Cutting board
- Chef's knife
- Wooden spoon or spatula
- Measuring cups and spoons

Fun Fact

Curry is a staple in many cuisines around the world, including Indian, Thai, and Caribbean. The term "curry" is derived from the Tamil word "kari," which means sauce.

SPINACH AND WHITE BEAN SOUP

Ingredients

- 1 tablespoon olive oil
- 1 onion, finely chopped
- 2 cloves garlic, minced
- 1 carrot, diced
- 1 celery stalk, diced
- 4 cups vegetable broth
- 1 can (15 oz) white beans, drained and rinsed
- 2 cups fresh spinach leaves
- 1 teaspoon dried thyme
- 1 teaspoon dried rosemary
- Salt and pepper to taste
- Fresh parsley, chopped (for garnish)

Instructions

1. Heat the olive oil in a large pot over medium heat.
2. Add the chopped onion, diced carrot, and diced celery. Sauté until softened, about 5-7 minutes.
3. Add the minced garlic and cook for another 1-2 minutes, until fragrant.
4. Stir in the vegetable broth, white beans, dried thyme, and dried rosemary.
5. Bring the soup to a simmer and cook for 10-15 minutes, until the vegetables are tender.
6. Stir in the fresh spinach leaves and cook until wilted, about 2 minutes.
7. Season with salt and pepper to taste.
8. Serve hot, garnished with chopped fresh parsley.

Tips & Tricks

- **Add Protein**: Add cooked chicken or sausage for extra protein.
- **Creamy Option**: For a creamier texture, use an immersion blender to partially blend the soup before adding the spinach.
- **Make Ahead**: This soup can be made ahead and stored in the refrigerator for up to 3 days or frozen for up to 3 months.

Tools Needed

- Large pot

- Cutting board
- Chef's knife
- Wooden spoon or spatula
- Measuring cups and spoons

Fun Fact

White beans, also known as cannellini beans, are rich in fiber and protein. They have been cultivated for thousands of years and are a staple in Mediterranean and Italian cuisine.

CHICKEN AND RICE SOUP

Ingredients

- 1 tablespoon olive oil
- 1 onion, finely chopped
- 2 cloves garlic, minced
- 2 carrots, diced
- 2 celery stalks, diced
- 4 cups chicken broth
- 1 cup cooked chicken breast, shredded
- 1 cup cooked rice
- 1 teaspoon dried thyme
- 1 teaspoon dried parsley
- Salt and pepper to taste
- Fresh parsley, chopped (for garnish)

Instructions

1. Heat the olive oil in a large pot over medium heat.
2. Add the chopped onion, diced carrots, and diced celery. Sauté until softened, about 5-7 minutes.
3. Add the minced garlic and cook for another 1-2 minutes, until fragrant.
4. Stir in the chicken broth, shredded chicken, cooked rice, dried thyme, and dried parsley.
5. Bring the soup to a simmer and cook for 10-15 minutes, until the vegetables are tender and the flavors have melded.
6. Season with salt and pepper to taste.
7. Serve hot, garnished with chopped fresh parsley.

Tips & Tricks

- **Make Ahead**: This soup can be made ahead and stored in the refrigerator for up to 3 days or frozen for up to 3 months.
- **Variation**: Use quinoa or barley instead of rice for a different texture.
- **Add Veggies**: Add spinach or kale during the last few minutes of cooking for added nutrition.

Tools Needed

- Large pot
- Cutting board
- Chef's knife

- Wooden spoon or spatula
- Measuring cups and spoons

Fun Fact

Chicken and rice soup is a classic comfort food that is enjoyed worldwide. It is not only delicious but also nourishing and easy to digest, making it a popular choice when feeling under the weather.

BROCCOLI CHEDDAR SOUP

Ingredients

- 1 tablespoon butter
- 1 onion, finely chopped
- 2 cloves garlic, minced
- 1 carrot, diced
- 2 cups broccoli florets
- 3 cups vegetable broth
- 1 cup milk
- 1 1/2 cups sharp cheddar cheese, grated
- 2 tablespoons all-purpose flour
- Salt and pepper to taste
- Fresh parsley, chopped (for garnish)

Instructions

1. In a large pot, melt the butter over medium heat.
2. Add the chopped onion and diced carrot. Sauté until softened, about 5-7 minutes.
3. Add the minced garlic and cook for another 1-2 minutes, until fragrant.
4. Stir in the flour and cook for 1-2 minutes to form a roux.
5. Gradually add the vegetable broth, stirring constantly to avoid lumps.
6. Add the broccoli florets and bring the soup to a simmer. Cook for 10-15 minutes, until the broccoli is tender.
7. Stir in the milk and grated cheddar cheese until the cheese is melted and the soup is creamy.
8. Season with salt and pepper to taste.
9. Serve hot, garnished with chopped fresh parsley.

Tips & Tricks

- **Blending**: For a smoother texture, use an immersion blender to partially or fully blend the soup before adding the cheese.
- **Add Protein**: Include cooked chicken or bacon for extra protein.
- **Make Ahead**: This soup can be made ahead and stored in the refrigerator for up to 3 days or frozen for up to 3 months.

Tools Needed

- Large pot
- Cutting board
- Chef's knife
- Wooden spoon or spatula
- Measuring cups and spoons
- Grater

Fun Fact

Broccoli cheddar soup is a popular comfort food in the United States, often served in bread bowls for an extra indulgent experience. Broccoli is also a nutritional powerhouse, packed with vitamins, minerals, and fiber.

ZUCCHINI NOODLE BOWL

Ingredients

- 2 medium zucchinis, spiralized into noodles
- 1 cup cherry tomatoes, halved
- 1/2 cup red bell pepper, thinly sliced
- 1/4 cup red onion, thinly sliced
- 1/4 cup fresh basil, chopped
- 2 tablespoons olive oil
- 1 tablespoon balsamic vinegar
- 1 clove garlic, minced
- Salt and pepper to taste
- Parmesan cheese, grated (optional)

Instructions

1. In a large bowl, combine the spiralized zucchini noodles, halved cherry tomatoes, thinly sliced red bell pepper, and thinly sliced red onion.
2. In a small bowl, whisk together the olive oil, balsamic vinegar, minced garlic, salt, and pepper.
3. Pour the dressing over the zucchini noodle mixture and toss to coat evenly.
4. Garnish with chopped fresh basil and grated Parmesan cheese, if using.
5. Serve immediately.

Tips & Tricks

- **Make Ahead**: Prepare the vegetables and dressing ahead of time and store them separately. Toss them together just before serving.
- **Add Protein**: Include grilled chicken, shrimp, or tofu for a protein boost.
- **Extra Flavor**: Add a sprinkle of red pepper flakes for a bit of heat.

Tools Needed

- Spiralizer or julienne peeler
- Cutting board
- Chef's knife
- Mixing bowls
- Small whisk
- Measuring cups and spoons

Fun Fact

Zucchini, also known as courgette, is a type of summer squash that is low in calories and high in nutrients. Spiralized zucchini noodles, often called "zoodles," are a popular low-carb alternative to traditional pasta.

FRUIT AND NUT MIX

Ingredients

- 1/2 cup almonds
- 1/2 cup walnuts
- 1/2 cup cashews
- 1/2 cup dried cranberries
- 1/2 cup raisins
- 1/2 cup dried apricots, chopped
- 1/4 cup pumpkin seeds
- 1/4 cup sunflower seeds

Instructions

1. In a large mixing bowl, combine the almonds, walnuts, cashews, dried cranberries, raisins, chopped dried

apricots, pumpkin seeds, and sunflower seeds.
2. Mix until all ingredients are evenly distributed.
3. Store the fruit and nut mix in an airtight container for up to 2 weeks.

Tips & Tricks

- **Customize**: Feel free to substitute your favorite nuts or dried fruits based on your preference.
- **Portion Control**: Divide the mix into individual portions using small containers or resealable bags for easy grab-and-go snacks.
- **Add Chocolate**: For a sweet treat, add a handful of dark chocolate chips or cocoa nibs.

Tools Needed

- Mixing bowl
- Measuring cups

Fun Fact

Nuts are a great source of healthy fats, protein, and fiber, while dried fruits provide natural sweetness and essential vitamins. This combination makes for a nutritious and satisfying snack.

YOGURT AND BERRY PARFAIT

Ingredients

- 1 cup Greek yogurt
- 1/2 cup mixed berries (strawberries, blueberries, raspberries)
- 1/4 cup granola
- 1 tablespoon honey (optional)
- Fresh mint leaves for garnish (optional)

Instructions

1. In a glass or bowl, add a layer of Greek yogurt.
2. Top the yogurt with a layer of mixed berries.
3. Add a layer of granola on top of the berries.
4. Repeat the layers until all ingredients are used, ending

with a layer of berries and granola on top.
5. Drizzle with honey, if desired.
6. Garnish with fresh mint leaves.
7. Serve immediately.

Tips & Tricks

- **Customize**: Use your favorite berries or substitute with other fruits like mango, banana, or kiwi.
- **Texture**: Add nuts or seeds for extra crunch and nutrition.
- **Make Ahead**: Assemble the parfaits in individual jars for an easy grab-and-go breakfast or snack.

Tools Needed

- Glass or bowl
- Spoon
- Measuring cups

Fun Fact

Greek yogurt is thicker and creamier than regular yogurt because it has been strained to remove most of its whey. It is also higher in protein and lower in sugar, making it a healthier choice.

VEGGIE STICKS WITH HUMMUS

Ingredients

- 1 cup baby carrots
- 1 cup cucumber sticks
- 1 cup bell pepper sticks (red, yellow, or green)
- 1 cup celery sticks
- 1 cup hummus (store-bought or homemade)

Instructions

1. Wash and peel the vegetables as needed.
2. Cut the cucumbers, bell peppers, and celery into sticks.
3. Arrange the baby carrots, cucumber sticks, bell pepper sticks, and celery sticks on a plate.
4. Place the hummus in a small bowl and set it in the

center of the plate.
5. Serve immediately.

Tips & Tricks

- **Variety**: Use a variety of colored bell peppers for a more visually appealing dish.
- **Flavor**: Try different flavors of hummus such as roasted red pepper, garlic, or spicy hummus.
- **Make Ahead**: Cut the veggies ahead of time and store them in airtight containers in the refrigerator for up to 3 days.

Tools Needed

- Cutting board
- Chef's knife
- Small bowl
- Plate for serving

Fun Fact

Hummus, made from chickpeas, tahini, lemon juice, and garlic, is a popular dip in Middle Eastern cuisine. It is rich in protein and fiber, making it a healthy and satisfying snack.

AVOCADO TOAST

Ingredients

- 2 slices whole grain bread
- 1 ripe avocado
- 1 tablespoon lemon juice
- Salt and pepper to taste
- Optional toppings: cherry tomatoes, radishes, red pepper flakes, olive oil, fresh herbs

Instructions

1. Toast the slices of whole grain bread until golden brown.
2. While the bread is toasting, cut the avocado in half, remove the pit, and scoop the flesh into a bowl.

3. Mash the avocado with a fork until smooth.
4. Add the lemon juice, salt, and pepper to the mashed avocado, and mix well.
5. Spread the avocado mixture evenly over the toasted bread slices.
6. Add any optional toppings you like, such as cherry tomatoes, radishes, red pepper flakes, a drizzle of olive oil, or fresh herbs.
7. Serve immediately.

Tips & Tricks

- **Make Ahead**: Prepare the mashed avocado mixture ahead of time and store it in an airtight container in the refrigerator. Just add lemon juice to prevent browning.
- **Extra Protein**: Top with a poached egg for an extra protein boost.
- **Flavor Boost**: Add a sprinkle of everything bagel seasoning for added flavor.

Tools Needed

- Toaster
- Knife
- Fork
- Bowl

Fun Fact

Avocado toast has become a popular breakfast and brunch item in recent years, but avocados have been enjoyed for centuries. They are native to Central and South America and were first cultivated by the Aztecs around 500 B.C.

COTTAGE CHEESE AND FRUIT

Ingredients

- 1 cup cottage cheese
- 1/2 cup mixed fresh fruit (strawberries, blueberries, pineapple, or your favorite fruits)
- 1 tablespoon honey (optional)
- Fresh mint leaves for garnish (optional)

Instructions

1. In a serving bowl, scoop the cottage cheese.
2. Top the cottage cheese with mixed fresh fruit.
3. Drizzle with honey, if desired.
4. Garnish with fresh mint leaves.
5. Serve immediately.

Tips & Tricks

- **Customize**: Use your favorite fruits or whatever is in season.
- **Add Crunch**: Sprinkle some granola or nuts on top for added texture and flavor.
- **Make Ahead**: Prepare the fruit ahead of time and store it in the refrigerator. Assemble just before serving.

Tools Needed

- Bowl
- Spoon
- Knife (for cutting fruit)

Fun Fact

Cottage cheese is a fresh cheese curd product with a mild flavor. It is high in protein and low in fat, making it a popular choice for health-conscious individuals. It has been enjoyed for centuries and was even a favorite of President Richard Nixon!

CHEESE AND WHOLE GRAIN CRACKERS

Ingredients

- 1 cup whole grain crackers
- 1/2 cup assorted cheese slices (cheddar, gouda, brie, etc.)
- Fresh grapes or apple slices (optional, for serving)
- Fresh herbs for garnish (optional)

Instructions

1. Arrange the whole grain crackers on a serving plate.
2. Place the assorted cheese slices next to the crackers.
3. Add fresh grapes or apple slices to the plate, if desired.
4. Garnish with fresh herbs, if desired.

5. Serve immediately.

Tips & Tricks

- **Cheese Variety**: Use a mix of your favorite cheeses to keep it interesting.
- **Add Protein**: Include slices of deli meat, such as turkey or ham, for added protein.
- **Make Ahead**: Pre-slice the cheese and store it in the refrigerator. Assemble the plate just before serving.

Tools Needed

- Serving plate
- Knife (for cutting cheese and fruit)

Fun Fact

Whole grain crackers are made with whole grains like wheat, oats, or rye, which retain all parts of the grain, providing more fiber and nutrients than refined grain products.

PEANUT BUTTER BANANA ROLL-UP

Ingredients

- 1 whole wheat tortilla
- 2 tablespoons peanut butter
- 1 banana
- 1 teaspoon honey (optional)
- Cinnamon (optional)

Instructions

1. Lay the whole wheat tortilla flat on a clean surface.
2. Spread the peanut butter evenly over the tortilla.
3. Place the banana on one edge of the tortilla.
4. Drizzle with honey and sprinkle with cinnamon, if desired.

5. Roll the tortilla tightly around the banana.
6. Cut the roll-up into slices or serve whole.

Tips & Tricks

- **Nut Alternatives**: Substitute peanut butter with almond butter or sunflower seed butter for a different flavor.
- **Add Crunch**: Sprinkle chopped nuts or granola over the peanut butter before rolling for added texture.
- **Make Ahead**: Prepare the roll-up and wrap it in plastic wrap for an easy grab-and-go snack.

Tools Needed

- Knife
- Spreading knife

Fun Fact

Bananas are a great source of potassium and vitamin C, while peanut butter provides protein and healthy fats, making this a nutritious and satisfying snack.

TRAIL MIX ENERGY BITES

Ingredients

- 1 cup rolled oats
- 1/2 cup peanut butter
- 1/4 cup honey
- 1/4 cup dried cranberries
- 1/4 cup chocolate chips
- 1/4 cup chopped nuts (almonds, walnuts, or pecans)
- 1 tablespoon chia seeds (optional)
- 1 teaspoon vanilla extract

Instructions

1. In a large mixing bowl, combine the rolled oats, peanut butter, honey, dried cranberries, chocolate chips,

chopped nuts, chia seeds (if using), and vanilla extract.
2. Mix until all ingredients are well combined.
3. Use a small cookie scoop or your hands to form the mixture into bite-sized balls.
4. Place the energy bites on a baking sheet lined with parchment paper.
5. Refrigerate for at least 30 minutes to firm up.
6. Store the energy bites in an airtight container in the refrigerator for up to 1 week.

Tips & Tricks

- **Customize**: Feel free to substitute your favorite dried fruits, nuts, or seeds.
- **No-Bake**: These energy bites require no baking, making them quick and easy to prepare.
- **Make Ahead**: Prepare a large batch and freeze them for a convenient grab-and-go snack.

Tools Needed

- Mixing bowl
- Small cookie scoop or hands
- Baking sheet
- Parchment paper

Fun Fact

Energy bites are a convenient and nutritious snack that combines the goodness of trail mix in a portable, bite-sized form. They are perfect for a quick energy boost during hikes, workouts, or busy days.

RICE CAKE WITH NUT BUTTER AND BANANA

Ingredients

- 1 rice cake
- 2 tablespoons nut butter (peanut butter, almond butter, or sunflower seed butter)
- 1 banana, sliced
- 1 teaspoon honey (optional)
- A pinch of cinnamon (optional)

Instructions

1. Spread the nut butter evenly over the rice cake.
2. Arrange the banana slices on top of the nut butter.
3. Drizzle with honey and sprinkle with cinnamon, if

desired.

4. Serve immediately.

Tips & Tricks

- **Nut Alternatives**: Use your favorite nut or seed butter for variety.
- **Add Crunch**: Sprinkle some chia seeds, flaxseeds, or granola on top for extra texture.
- **Make Ahead**: Prepare the ingredients ahead of time and assemble just before eating for maximum freshness.

Tools Needed

- Knife
- Spreading knife

Fun Fact

Rice cakes are a popular snack in many cultures and are known for their low-calorie content. Combined with nut butter and banana, they make a balanced and satisfying snack that provides both quick and sustained energy.

CHICKEN AND HUMMUS PLATE

Ingredients

- 1 cup cooked chicken breast, sliced
- 1/2 cup hummus (store-bought or homemade)
- 1/2 cup cherry tomatoes, halved
- 1/2 cucumber, sliced
- 1/4 cup Kalamata olives
- 1/4 cup feta cheese, crumbled
- 1 tablespoon olive oil
- Fresh parsley, chopped (for garnish)
- Salt and pepper to taste

Instructions

1. Arrange the sliced chicken breast, hummus, cherry

tomatoes, cucumber slices, Kalamata olives, and crumbled feta cheese on a plate.
2. Drizzle olive oil over the hummus and sprinkle with salt and pepper to taste.
3. Garnish with chopped fresh parsley.
4. Serve immediately.

Tips & Tricks

- **Make Ahead**: Prepare all the ingredients ahead of time and store them separately in the refrigerator. Assemble the plate just before serving.
- **Add Variety**: Include other fresh vegetables like bell peppers, carrots, or radishes.
- **Flavor Boost**: Add a squeeze of lemon juice over the chicken for extra flavor.

Tools Needed

- Cutting board
- Chef's knife
- Plate for serving

Fun Fact

Hummus is a popular Middle Eastern dip made from chickpeas, tahini, lemon juice, and garlic. It is rich in protein and fiber, making it a healthy and satisfying addition to any meal.

TURKEY AND CHEESE ROLL-UPS

Ingredients

- 4 slices deli turkey breast
- 4 slices cheese (cheddar, Swiss, or your favorite)
- 1/4 cup cream cheese, softened
- 1/4 cup baby spinach leaves
- 1/4 cup bell pepper strips (red, yellow, or green)

Instructions

1. Lay a slice of turkey breast flat on a clean surface.
2. Spread a thin layer of cream cheese over the turkey slice.
3. Place a slice of cheese on top of the turkey.
4. Add a few spinach leaves and bell pepper strips at one

end of the turkey slice.

5. Roll the turkey tightly from the end with the vegetables to the opposite end.
6. Repeat with the remaining ingredients.
7. Cut each roll-up in half or serve whole.

Tips & Tricks

- **Make Ahead**: Prepare the roll-ups ahead of time and store them in an airtight container in the refrigerator for up to 2 days.
- **Add Crunch**: Include a few cucumber sticks or carrot sticks for added crunch.
- **Dipping Sauce**: Serve with a side of mustard or ranch dressing for extra flavor.

Tools Needed

- Cutting board
- Knife
- Spreading knife

Fun Fact

Turkey and cheese roll-ups are a versatile and protein-packed snack that can be customized with your favorite veggies and cheeses. They are perfect for a quick lunch or an on-the-go snack.

HARD-BOILED EGGS AND VEGGIE PLATE

Ingredients

- 2 hard-boiled eggs, peeled and halved
- 1 cup baby carrots
- 1 cup cucumber slices
- 1 cup cherry tomatoes
- 1/4 cup hummus (store-bought or homemade)
- Salt and pepper to taste
- Fresh herbs for garnish (optional)

Instructions

1. Arrange the hard-boiled egg halves, baby carrots, cucumber slices, and cherry tomatoes on a plate.

2. Place the hummus in a small bowl and set it on the plate.
3. Season the hard-boiled eggs with salt and pepper to taste.
4. Garnish with fresh herbs, if desired.
5. Serve immediately.

Tips & Tricks

- **Variety**: Add other fresh vegetables like bell pepper strips, celery sticks, or radishes for more variety.
- **Make Ahead**: Prepare the hard-boiled eggs and vegetables ahead of time and store them in the refrigerator. Assemble the plate just before serving.
- **Dipping Sauce**: Include other dips like ranch or tzatziki for more dipping options.

Tools Needed

- Cutting board
- Knife
- Plate for serving
- Small bowl

Fun Fact

Hard-boiled eggs are a great source of high-quality protein and essential vitamins and minerals. Paired with fresh veggies and hummus, they make for a nutritious and satisfying snack or light meal.

EDAMAME AND QUINOA BOWL

Ingredients

- 1 cup cooked quinoa
- 1/2 cup shelled edamame (cooked)
- 1/2 cup cherry tomatoes, halved
- 1/2 avocado, diced
- 1/4 cup shredded carrots
- 1/4 cup cucumber, diced
- 2 tablespoons soy sauce or tamari
- 1 tablespoon sesame oil
- 1 tablespoon rice vinegar
- 1 teaspoon sesame seeds
- Fresh cilantro or green onions for garnish (optional)

Instructions

1. In a large bowl, combine the cooked quinoa, shelled edamame, cherry tomatoes, diced avocado, shredded carrots, and diced cucumber.
2. In a small bowl, whisk together the soy sauce or tamari, sesame oil, and rice vinegar.
3. Pour the dressing over the quinoa and vegetable mixture and toss to coat evenly.
4. Sprinkle with sesame seeds and garnish with fresh cilantro or green onions, if desired.
5. Serve immediately.

Tips & Tricks

- **Make Ahead**: Prepare the quinoa and chop the vegetables ahead of time. Store them separately in the refrigerator and assemble the bowl just before serving.
- **Add Protein**: Include grilled chicken, tofu, or shrimp for additional protein.
- **Flavor Boost**: Add a squeeze of lime juice or a pinch of red pepper flakes for extra flavor.

Tools Needed

- Cutting board
- Chef's knife
- Mixing bowls
- Small whisk
- Measuring cups and spoons

Fun Fact

Edamame are young soybeans that are packed with protein, fiber, and essential nutrients. They have been a staple in East Asian cuisine for centuries and are often enjoyed as a healthy snack or addition to salads and bowls.

SHRIMP AND AVOCADO SALAD

Ingredients

- 1 cup cooked shrimp, peeled and deveined
- 1 avocado, diced
- 1 cup cherry tomatoes, halved
- 1/4 red onion, finely chopped
- 1/4 cup fresh cilantro, chopped
- 2 tablespoons lime juice
- 1 tablespoon olive oil
- Salt and pepper to taste

Instructions

1. In a large mixing bowl, combine the cooked shrimp, diced avocado, halved cherry tomatoes, finely chopped

red onion, and chopped fresh cilantro.

2. In a small bowl, whisk together the lime juice, olive oil, salt, and pepper.
3. Pour the dressing over the shrimp and avocado mixture and toss gently to coat.
4. Serve immediately or refrigerate for up to 1 hour before serving.

Tips & Tricks

- **Make Ahead**: Prepare all ingredients ahead of time and store them separately in the refrigerator. Assemble the salad just before serving.
- **Extra Flavor**: Add a pinch of red pepper flakes or a dash of hot sauce for a spicy kick.
- **Variations**: Substitute shrimp with grilled chicken or tofu for a different protein option.

Tools Needed

- Cutting board
- Chef's knife
- Mixing bowl
- Small whisk
- Measuring cups and spoons

Fun Fact

Shrimp is a low-calorie, high-protein seafood that is rich in nutrients such as selenium, vitamin B12, and phosphorus. Combined with avocado, which is high in healthy fats, this salad is both nutritious and delicious.

GREEK YOGURT CHICKEN SALAD

Ingredients

- 2 cups cooked chicken breast, shredded
- 1/2 cup Greek yogurt
- 1/4 cup mayonnaise
- 1/4 cup celery, finely chopped
- 1/4 cup red onion, finely chopped
- 1/4 cup grapes, halved
- 1/4 cup chopped walnuts (optional)
- 1 tablespoon Dijon mustard
- 1 tablespoon lemon juice
- Salt and pepper to taste
- Fresh parsley, chopped (for garnish)

Instructions

1. In a large mixing bowl, combine the shredded chicken, Greek yogurt, mayonnaise, finely chopped celery, finely chopped red onion, halved grapes, and chopped walnuts (if using).
2. Add the Dijon mustard, lemon juice, salt, and pepper. Mix until all ingredients are well combined.
3. Taste and adjust seasoning if necessary.
4. Serve immediately or refrigerate for at least 30 minutes to allow flavors to meld.
5. Garnish with chopped fresh parsley before serving.

Tips & Tricks

- **Make Ahead**: This salad can be made ahead and stored in the refrigerator for up to 3 days.
- **Add Crunch**: Include chopped apples or cucumbers for extra crunch.
- **Serving Suggestions**: Serve on a bed of lettuce, in a sandwich, or with whole grain crackers.

Tools Needed

- Mixing bowl
- Chef's knife
- Measuring cups and spoons

Fun Fact

Greek yogurt is a great substitute for mayonnaise, offering a creamy texture with less fat and more protein. It's a healthier option that still provides rich flavor and creaminess.

BEEF AND VEGGIE STIR-FRY

Ingredients

- 1 lb beef sirloin, thinly sliced
- 2 tablespoons soy sauce
- 1 tablespoon oyster sauce
- 1 tablespoon hoisin sauce
- 1 tablespoon cornstarch
- 2 tablespoons vegetable oil
- 1 cup broccoli florets
- 1 bell pepper, sliced
- 1 carrot, julienned
- 1/2 cup snap peas
- 2 cloves garlic, minced
- 1 tablespoon ginger, grated

- 1/4 cup green onions, chopped
- 1 tablespoon sesame seeds (optional)
- Salt and pepper to taste

Instructions

1. In a bowl, combine the thinly sliced beef, soy sauce, oyster sauce, hoisin sauce, and cornstarch. Mix well and let it marinate for at least 15 minutes.
2. Heat 1 tablespoon of vegetable oil in a large skillet or wok over medium-high heat.
3. Add the marinated beef to the skillet and stir-fry until browned, about 3-4 minutes. Remove the beef from the skillet and set aside.
4. In the same skillet, add the remaining 1 tablespoon of vegetable oil.
5. Add the broccoli florets, sliced bell pepper, julienned carrot, and snap peas. Stir-fry for 4-5 minutes, until the vegetables are tender but still crisp.
6. Add the minced garlic and grated ginger to the skillet and stir-fry for another 1-2 minutes, until fragrant.
7. Return the beef to the skillet and mix well with the vegetables.
8. Season with salt and pepper to taste.
9. Garnish with chopped green onions and sesame seeds, if desired.
10. Serve immediately.

Tips & Tricks

- **Make Ahead**: Marinate the beef ahead of time and store

it in the refrigerator until ready to cook.

- **Add Spice**: Add a pinch of red pepper flakes or a dash of hot sauce for extra heat.
- **Serving Suggestion**: Serve over steamed rice or noodles for a complete meal.

Tools Needed

- Cutting board
- Chef's knife
- Large skillet or wok
- Mixing bowl
- Wooden spoon or spatula
- Measuring cups and spoons

Fun Fact

Stir-frying is a quick and healthy cooking method that originated in China. It involves cooking ingredients quickly over high heat, which helps retain their nutrients and vibrant colors.

BLACK BEAN AND CORN SALAD

Ingredients

- 1 can (15 oz) black beans, drained and rinsed
- 1 cup corn kernels (fresh, frozen, or canned)
- 1 red bell pepper, diced
- 1/4 red onion, finely chopped
- 1/4 cup fresh cilantro, chopped
- 1 avocado, diced
- 1 tablespoon lime juice
- 1 tablespoon olive oil
- 1 teaspoon ground cumin
- Salt and pepper to taste

Instructions

1. In a large mixing bowl, combine the black beans, corn kernels, diced red bell pepper, finely chopped red onion, and chopped fresh cilantro.
2. In a small bowl, whisk together the lime juice, olive oil, ground cumin, salt, and pepper.
3. Pour the dressing over the black bean mixture and toss to coat evenly.
4. Gently fold in the diced avocado.
5. Serve immediately or refrigerate for up to 1 hour before serving.

Tips & Tricks

- **Make Ahead**: Prepare the salad ahead of time and store it in the refrigerator. Add the avocado just before serving to prevent browning.
- **Add Protein**: Include grilled chicken or shrimp for added protein.
- **Extra Flavor**: Add a dash of hot sauce or a sprinkle of feta cheese for extra flavor.

Tools Needed

- Cutting board
- Chef's knife
- Mixing bowls
- Small whisk
- Measuring cups and spoons

Fun Fact

Black beans are a staple in Latin American cuisine and are known for their high fiber and protein content. They pair well with corn, creating a colorful and nutritious salad.

SALMON AND ASPARAGUS SALAD

Ingredients

- 1 cup cooked salmon, flaked
- 1 bunch asparagus, trimmed and cut into 2-inch pieces
- 1 cup cherry tomatoes, halved
- 1/4 red onion, thinly sliced
- 1/4 cup fresh dill, chopped
- 2 tablespoons lemon juice
- 2 tablespoons olive oil
- Salt and pepper to taste
- Lemon wedges for serving

Instructions

1. Bring a pot of water to a boil. Add the asparagus

and cook for 2-3 minutes until tender-crisp. Drain and rinse with cold water to stop the cooking process.

2. In a large mixing bowl, combine the flaked salmon, cooked asparagus, halved cherry tomatoes, and thinly sliced red onion.
3. In a small bowl, whisk together the lemon juice, olive oil, salt, and pepper.
4. Pour the dressing over the salad and toss gently to coat.
5. Garnish with chopped fresh dill.
6. Serve immediately with lemon wedges on the side.

Tips & Tricks

- **Make Ahead**: Prepare the salad ingredients ahead of time and store them separately in the refrigerator. Assemble the salad just before serving.
- **Add Flavor**: Include a pinch of red pepper flakes or capers for extra flavor.
- **Serving Suggestion**: Serve on a bed of mixed greens for a more substantial meal.

Tools Needed

- Cutting board
- Chef's knife
- Mixing bowls
- Small whisk
- Measuring cups and spoons

Fun Fact

Salmon is a rich source of omega-3 fatty acids, which are beneficial for heart health. Asparagus is high in vitamins A, C, and K, making this salad both nutritious and delicious.

TOFU AND VEGGIE STIR-FRY

Ingredients

- 1 block (14 oz) firm tofu, drained and cubed
- 2 tablespoons soy sauce
- 1 tablespoon sesame oil
- 1 tablespoon olive oil
- 1 cup broccoli florets
- 1 red bell pepper, sliced
- 1 carrot, julienned
- 1 cup snap peas
- 2 cloves garlic, minced
- 1 tablespoon grated ginger
- 1/4 cup green onions, chopped
- 1 tablespoon sesame seeds (optional)

- Salt and pepper to taste

Instructions

1. In a small bowl, mix the cubed tofu with 1 tablespoon of soy sauce. Let it marinate for 10 minutes.
2. Heat the sesame oil and olive oil in a large skillet or wok over medium-high heat.
3. Add the marinated tofu to the skillet and cook until browned on all sides, about 5-7 minutes. Remove the tofu from the skillet and set aside.
4. In the same skillet, add the broccoli florets, sliced red bell pepper, julienned carrot, and snap peas. Stir-fry for 4-5 minutes, until the vegetables are tender but still crisp.
5. Add the minced garlic and grated ginger to the skillet and stir-fry for another 1-2 minutes, until fragrant.
6. Return the tofu to the skillet and mix well with the vegetables.
7. Add the remaining 1 tablespoon of soy sauce and stir to coat evenly.
8. Season with salt and pepper to taste.
9. Garnish with chopped green onions and sesame seeds, if desired.
10. Serve immediately.

Tips & Tricks

- **Make Ahead**: Press and marinate the tofu ahead of time for quicker preparation.
- **Add Spice**: Include a pinch of red pepper flakes or a

dash of sriracha for extra heat.
- **Serving Suggestion**: Serve over steamed rice or noodles for a complete meal.

Tools Needed

- Cutting board
- Chef's knife
- Large skillet or wok
- Mixing bowl
- Wooden spoon or spatula
- Measuring cups and spoons

Fun Fact

Tofu, also known as bean curd, is made from soy milk and is a staple in East Asian and Southeast Asian cuisines. It is a great source of protein and can absorb the flavors of the ingredients it is cooked with.

VEGAN LENTIL SALAD

Ingredients

- 1 cup cooked green or brown lentils
- 1/2 cup cherry tomatoes, halved
- 1/2 cucumber, diced
- 1/4 red onion, finely chopped
- 1/4 cup fresh parsley, chopped
- 1/4 cup fresh mint, chopped
- 2 tablespoons olive oil
- 2 tablespoons lemon juice
- 1 teaspoon Dijon mustard
- Salt and pepper to taste

Instructions

1. In a large mixing bowl, combine the cooked lentils, halved cherry tomatoes, diced cucumber, finely chopped red onion, chopped parsley, and chopped mint.
2. In a small bowl, whisk together the olive oil, lemon juice, Dijon mustard, salt, and pepper.
3. Pour the dressing over the lentil mixture and toss to coat evenly.
4. Serve immediately or refrigerate for up to 1 hour before serving.

Tips & Tricks

- **Make Ahead**: Prepare the salad ahead of time and store it in the refrigerator. The flavors will meld and improve over time.
- **Add Protein**: Include cooked quinoa or chickpeas for added protein.
- **Flavor Boost**: Add a sprinkle of feta cheese (if not strictly vegan) or a dash of hot sauce for extra flavor.

Tools Needed

- Cutting board
- Chef's knife
- Mixing bowls
- Small whisk
- Measuring cups and spoons

Fun Fact

Lentils are one of the oldest cultivated crops, dating back to 8,000 B.C. They are a great source of protein, fiber, and essential nutrients, making them a staple in many diets around the world.

VEGETARIAN STUFFED PEPPERS

Ingredients

- 4 bell peppers (any color), tops cut off and seeds removed
- 1 cup cooked quinoa or rice
- 1 can (15 oz) black beans, drained and rinsed
- 1 cup corn kernels (fresh or canned)
- 1 cup diced tomatoes
- 1/2 cup shredded cheese (optional for vegan)
- 1/4 cup chopped fresh cilantro
- 1 teaspoon cumin
- 1 teaspoon chili powder
- Salt and pepper to taste
- 1 tablespoon olive oil

- Fresh lime wedges for serving

Instructions

1. Preheat your oven to 375°F (190°C).
2. In a large mixing bowl, combine the cooked quinoa or rice, black beans, corn kernels, diced tomatoes, shredded cheese (if using), chopped fresh cilantro, cumin, chili powder, salt, and pepper.
3. Stuff the bell peppers with the quinoa mixture, pressing down gently to fill them completely.
4. Place the stuffed peppers in a baking dish and drizzle with olive oil.
5. Cover the dish with aluminum foil and bake for 30 minutes.
6. Remove the foil and bake for an additional 10-15 minutes, until the peppers are tender and the tops are slightly browned.
7. Serve immediately with fresh lime wedges on the side.

Tips & Tricks

- **Make Ahead**: Prepare the stuffing mixture ahead of time and store it in the refrigerator. Stuff the peppers just before baking.
- **Add Protein**: Include cooked lentils or tofu for added protein.
- **Flavor Boost**: Add a dash of hot sauce or a sprinkle of feta cheese for extra flavor.

Tools Needed

- Cutting board
- Chef's knife
- Mixing bowl
- Baking dish
- Measuring cups and spoons

Fun Fact

Stuffed peppers are a versatile dish found in many cuisines around the world, including Mediterranean, Middle Eastern, and Latin American. They can be filled with a variety of ingredients, making them a perfect canvas for creative cooking.

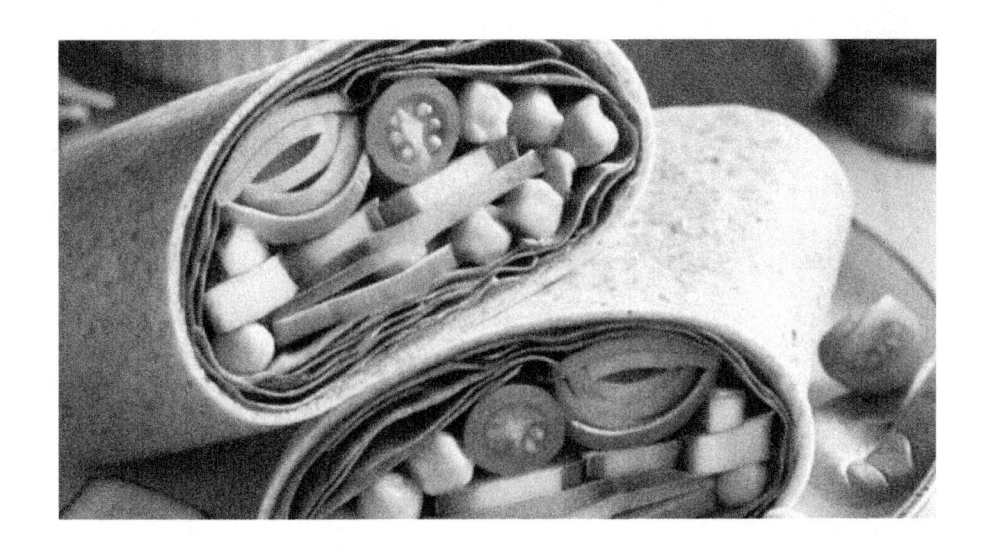

CHICKPEA AND SPINACH WRAP

Ingredients

- 1 can (15 oz) chickpeas, drained and rinsed
- 1 cup fresh spinach leaves
- 1/4 cup red onion, thinly sliced
- 1/4 cup cherry tomatoes, halved
- 1/4 cup cucumber, diced
- 2 tablespoons hummus
- 1 tablespoon olive oil
- 1 tablespoon lemon juice
- 1 teaspoon ground cumin
- Salt and pepper to taste
- 2 whole wheat tortillas

Instructions

1. In a mixing bowl, combine the chickpeas, spinach leaves, thinly sliced red onion, halved cherry tomatoes, and diced cucumber.
2. In a small bowl, whisk together the hummus, olive oil, lemon juice, ground cumin, salt, and pepper.
3. Pour the dressing over the chickpea mixture and toss to coat evenly.
4. Lay the whole wheat tortillas flat on a clean surface.
5. Divide the chickpea and spinach mixture between the two tortillas, placing it in the center of each tortilla.
6. Fold the sides of the tortilla over the filling, then roll it up tightly from the bottom to the top.
7. Cut the wraps in half and serve immediately.

Tips & Tricks

- **Make Ahead**: Prepare the chickpea and spinach mixture ahead of time and store it in the refrigerator. Assemble the wraps just before serving.
- **Add Protein**: Include grilled tofu or tempeh for added protein.
- **Flavor Boost**: Add a pinch of red pepper flakes or a drizzle of hot sauce for extra flavor.

Tools Needed

- Cutting board
- Chef's knife

- Mixing bowls
- Small whisk
- Measuring cups and spoons

Fun Fact

Chickpeas, also known as garbanzo beans, are a great source of plant-based protein and fiber. They have been cultivated in the Middle East for thousands of years and are a staple in many cuisines.

AVOCADO AND BLACK BEAN SALAD

Ingredients

- 1 can (15 oz) black beans, drained and rinsed
- 1 avocado, diced
- 1 cup cherry tomatoes, halved
- 1/4 red onion, finely chopped
- 1/4 cup fresh cilantro, chopped
- 1 tablespoon lime juice
- 1 tablespoon olive oil
- Salt and pepper to taste

Instructions

1. In a large mixing bowl, combine the black beans, diced avocado, halved cherry tomatoes, finely chopped red

onion, and chopped fresh cilantro.

2. In a small bowl, whisk together the lime juice, olive oil, salt, and pepper.
3. Pour the dressing over the black bean mixture and toss gently to coat.
4. Serve immediately or refrigerate for up to 1 hour before serving.

Tips & Tricks

- **Make Ahead**: Prepare the salad ahead of time and store it in the refrigerator. Add the avocado just before serving to prevent browning.
- **Add Protein**: Include grilled chicken or shrimp for added protein.
- **Extra Flavor**: Add a dash of hot sauce or a sprinkle of feta cheese for extra flavor.

Tools Needed

- Cutting board
- Chef's knife
- Mixing bowls
- Small whisk
- Measuring cups and spoons

Fun Fact

Avocados are rich in healthy monounsaturated fats, which are good for heart health. They also contain more potassium than bananas!

VEGAN BUDDHA BOWL

Ingredients

- 1 cup cooked quinoa or brown rice
- 1 cup chickpeas, drained and rinsed
- 1 cup roasted sweet potatoes, diced
- 1 cup broccoli florets, steamed
- 1/2 avocado, sliced
- 1/4 cup shredded carrots
- 1/4 cup red cabbage, thinly sliced
- 2 tablespoons tahini
- 1 tablespoon lemon juice
- 1 tablespoon olive oil
- 1 teaspoon maple syrup
- 1 clove garlic, minced

- Salt and pepper to taste
- Sesame seeds (optional, for garnish)
- Fresh cilantro or parsley (optional, for garnish)

Instructions

1. In a bowl, arrange the cooked quinoa or brown rice as the base.
2. Top with chickpeas, roasted sweet potatoes, steamed broccoli, sliced avocado, shredded carrots, and thinly sliced red cabbage.
3. In a small bowl, whisk together the tahini, lemon juice, olive oil, maple syrup, minced garlic, salt, and pepper to make the dressing.
4. Drizzle the dressing over the Buddha bowl.
5. Garnish with sesame seeds and fresh cilantro or parsley, if desired.
6. Serve immediately.

Tips & Tricks

- **Make Ahead**: Prepare the quinoa, chickpeas, and vegetables ahead of time and store them in the refrigerator. Assemble the bowl just before serving.
- **Add Protein**: Include grilled tofu or tempeh for added protein.
- **Flavor Boost**: Add a dash of hot sauce or a sprinkle of nutritional yeast for extra flavor.

Tools Needed

- Cutting board
- Chef's knife
- Mixing bowls
- Small whisk
- Measuring cups and spoons

Fun Fact

Buddha bowls are named for their "rounded" appearance, resembling a Buddha's belly. They are typically a balanced meal in a bowl, including grains, protein, and a variety of colorful vegetables.

VEGETARIAN PASTA SALAD

Ingredients

- 2 cups cooked pasta (rotini, penne, or your favorite)
- 1 cup cherry tomatoes, halved
- 1/2 cup cucumber, diced
- 1/2 cup bell peppers, diced (any color)
- 1/4 red onion, finely chopped
- 1/4 cup black olives, sliced
- 1/4 cup feta cheese, crumbled (optional for vegan)
- 1/4 cup fresh basil, chopped
- 2 tablespoons olive oil
- 1 tablespoon red wine vinegar
- 1 teaspoon Dijon mustard
- 1 clove garlic, minced

- Salt and pepper to taste

Instructions

1. In a large mixing bowl, combine the cooked pasta, halved cherry tomatoes, diced cucumber, diced bell peppers, finely chopped red onion, sliced black olives, crumbled feta cheese (if using), and chopped fresh basil.
2. In a small bowl, whisk together the olive oil, red wine vinegar, Dijon mustard, minced garlic, salt, and pepper.
3. Pour the dressing over the pasta salad and toss to coat evenly.
4. Serve immediately or refrigerate for up to 1 hour before serving.

Tips & Tricks

- **Make Ahead**: Prepare the pasta salad ahead of time and store it in the refrigerator. The flavors will meld and improve over time.
- **Add Protein**: Include chickpeas or grilled tofu for added protein.
- **Flavor Boost**: Add a dash of hot sauce or a sprinkle of nutritional yeast for extra flavor.

Tools Needed

- Cutting board
- Chef's knife
- Mixing bowls

- Small whisk
- Measuring cups and spoons

Fun Fact

Pasta salad is a versatile dish that can be customized with a variety of vegetables, proteins, and dressings. It is a popular choice for picnics, barbecues, and potlucks.

VEGAN TACOS

Ingredients

- 1 can (15 oz) black beans, drained and rinsed
- 1 cup corn kernels (fresh, frozen, or canned)
- 1 cup cherry tomatoes, halved
- 1/4 red onion, finely chopped
- 1 avocado, diced
- 1/4 cup fresh cilantro, chopped
- 1 tablespoon lime juice
- 1 tablespoon olive oil
- 1 teaspoon ground cumin
- 1 teaspoon chili powder
- Salt and pepper to taste
- 8 small corn tortillas

- Lime wedges for serving

Instructions

1. In a large mixing bowl, combine the black beans, corn kernels, halved cherry tomatoes, finely chopped red onion, diced avocado, and chopped fresh cilantro.
2. In a small bowl, whisk together the lime juice, olive oil, ground cumin, chili powder, salt, and pepper.
3. Pour the dressing over the bean mixture and toss to coat evenly.
4. Heat the corn tortillas in a dry skillet over medium heat until warm and pliable, about 1 minute per side.
5. Divide the bean mixture evenly among the tortillas.
6. Serve the tacos immediately with lime wedges on the side.

Tips & Tricks

- **Make Ahead**: Prepare the bean mixture ahead of time and store it in the refrigerator. Assemble the tacos just before serving.
- **Add Protein**: Include grilled tofu or tempeh for added protein.
- **Flavor Boost**: Add a dash of hot sauce or a sprinkle of nutritional yeast for extra flavor.

Tools Needed

- Cutting board
- Chef's knife

- Mixing bowls
- Small whisk
- Measuring cups and spoons
- Skillet

Fun Fact

Tacos are a traditional Mexican dish that dates back to ancient times. They are incredibly versatile and can be filled with a variety of ingredients, making them a favorite around the world.

GRILLED VEGGIE SANDWICH

Ingredients

- 1 zucchini, sliced lengthwise
- 1 red bell pepper, sliced
- 1 yellow bell pepper, sliced
- 1 red onion, sliced
- 4 slices of whole grain bread
- 2 tablespoons olive oil
- 1 tablespoon balsamic vinegar
- 1/4 cup hummus
- Salt and pepper to taste
- Fresh basil leaves (optional)

Instructions

1. Preheat a grill or grill pan over medium-high heat.
2. In a mixing bowl, toss the zucchini, red bell pepper, yellow bell pepper, and red onion slices with olive oil, balsamic vinegar, salt, and pepper.
3. Grill the vegetables for 3-4 minutes per side, until tender and slightly charred.
4. While the vegetables are grilling, toast the whole grain bread slices until golden brown.
5. Spread hummus on one side of each slice of bread.
6. Layer the grilled vegetables on two slices of the bread.
7. Add fresh basil leaves, if using.
8. Top with the remaining bread slices, hummus side down.
9. Cut the sandwiches in half and serve immediately.

Tips & Tricks

- **Make Ahead**: Grill the vegetables ahead of time and store them in the refrigerator. Assemble the sandwich just before serving.
- **Add Protein**: Include grilled tofu or tempeh for added protein.
- **Flavor Boost**: Add a sprinkle of feta cheese or a drizzle of hot sauce for extra flavor.

Tools Needed

- Cutting board
- Chef's knife
- Grill or grill pan

- Mixing bowl
- Spatula

Fun Fact

Grilling vegetables enhances their natural sweetness and adds a delicious smoky flavor. This sandwich is a great way to enjoy a variety of colorful, nutrient-rich veggies.

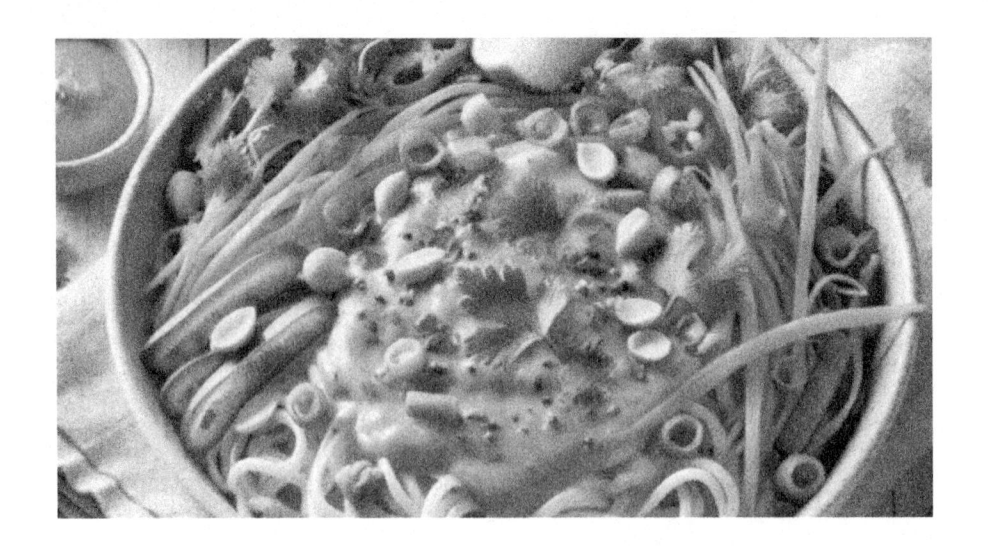

SPICY PEANUT NOODLES

Ingredients

- 8 oz rice noodles or spaghetti
- 1/4 cup peanut butter
- 2 tablespoons soy sauce
- 1 tablespoon rice vinegar
- 1 tablespoon sesame oil
- 1 tablespoon honey or maple syrup
- 1-2 teaspoons sriracha or chili garlic sauce (adjust to taste)
- 1 clove garlic, minced
- 1 teaspoon grated ginger
- 1/4 cup warm water
- 1 cup shredded carrots

- 1 cup bell pepper, thinly sliced
- 1/4 cup chopped green onions
- 1/4 cup chopped peanuts (optional for garnish)
- Fresh cilantro (optional for garnish)
- Lime wedges for serving

Instructions

1. Cook the noodles according to package instructions. Drain and set aside.
2. In a mixing bowl, whisk together the peanut butter, soy sauce, rice vinegar, sesame oil, honey or maple syrup, sriracha, minced garlic, grated ginger, and warm water until smooth.
3. In a large mixing bowl, combine the cooked noodles, shredded carrots, and sliced bell pepper.
4. Pour the peanut sauce over the noodles and vegetables. Toss to coat evenly.
5. Garnish with chopped green onions, chopped peanuts, and fresh cilantro, if using.
6. Serve immediately with lime wedges on the side.

Tips & Tricks

- **Make Ahead**: Prepare the peanut sauce ahead of time and store it in the refrigerator. Cook the noodles and assemble the dish just before serving.
- **Add Protein**: Include grilled tofu, chicken, or shrimp for added protein.
- **Extra Crunch**: Add chopped cucumber or snap peas for

extra crunch and freshness.

Tools Needed

- Pot for cooking noodles
- Mixing bowls
- Whisk
- Measuring cups and spoons
- Cutting board
- Chef's knife

Fun Fact

Peanut noodles are a popular dish in many Southeast Asian cuisines. The combination of creamy peanut sauce with fresh vegetables and noodles makes for a satisfying and flavorful meal.

VEGAN BURRITO BOWL

Ingredients

- 1 cup cooked brown rice or quinoa
- 1 can (15 oz) black beans, drained and rinsed
- 1 cup corn kernels (fresh, frozen, or canned)
- 1 cup cherry tomatoes, halved
- 1/2 red onion, finely chopped
- 1 avocado, diced
- 1/4 cup fresh cilantro, chopped
- 1/4 cup salsa
- 2 tablespoons lime juice
- 1 tablespoon olive oil
- 1 teaspoon ground cumin
- 1 teaspoon chili powder

- Salt and pepper to taste
- Lime wedges for serving

Instructions

1. In a large mixing bowl, combine the cooked brown rice or quinoa, black beans, corn kernels, halved cherry tomatoes, finely chopped red onion, diced avocado, and chopped fresh cilantro.
2. In a small bowl, whisk together the salsa, lime juice, olive oil, ground cumin, chili powder, salt, and pepper.
3. Pour the dressing over the burrito bowl mixture and toss gently to coat.
4. Serve immediately with lime wedges on the side.

Tips & Tricks

- **Make Ahead**: Prepare the ingredients ahead of time and store them in the refrigerator. Assemble the bowl just before serving.
- **Add Protein**: Include grilled tofu or tempeh for added protein.
- **Flavor Boost**: Add a dash of hot sauce or a sprinkle of nutritional yeast for extra flavor.

Tools Needed

- Cutting board
- Chef's knife
- Mixing bowls
- Small whisk

- Measuring cups and spoons

Fun Fact

Burrito bowls are a deconstructed version of the traditional burrito, offering all the flavors and ingredients without the tortilla. They are a versatile and healthy meal option that can be customized to your liking.

QUICK AND EASY MEAL PREP

Planning Ahead

1. **Create a Weekly Menu**: Plan your meals for the week, including breakfast, lunch, dinner, and snacks. Write down the recipes and make a shopping list of all the ingredients you'll need.

2. **Choose Simple Recipes**: Select recipes that are quick to prepare and use common ingredients. Look for meals that can be cooked in large batches and stored for later.

3. **Set Aside Time for Prep**: Dedicate a specific time each week for meal prep. This could be a few hours on Sunday or split across a couple of days. Consistency will help make meal prepping a habit.

Prepping Ingredients

1. **Wash and Chop Vegetables**: Clean and cut vegetables ahead of time. Store them in airtight containers in the refrigerator. This saves time during the week and makes it easier to assemble meals quickly.

2. **Cook Grains and Proteins**: Prepare large batches of grains like rice, quinoa, or pasta, and cook proteins such as chicken, tofu, or beans. Store them in separate containers for easy mix-and-match meals.

3. **Portion Out Snacks**: Divide snacks like nuts, fruits, and yogurt into single-serving portions. This makes it easy to grab a healthy snack on the go and helps with portion control.

Storing And Reheating Tips

1. **Use Quality Containers**: Invest in good-quality, airtight containers to keep your food fresh. Glass containers are great for reheating in the microwave or oven, while plastic containers are lightweight and easy to transport.

2. **Label and Date**: Label each container with the name of the dish and the date it was prepared. This helps you keep track of what needs to be eaten first and avoids food waste.

3. **Reheat Safely**: When reheating meals, ensure they reach an internal temperature of at least 165°F (74°C) to kill any harmful bacteria. Stir food halfway through reheating to ensure even heating.

Benefits Of Meal Prep

- **Saves Time**: Prepping meals ahead of time reduces the daily cooking time, allowing you to focus on other activities.

- **Saves Money**: Planning meals and buying ingredients in bulk can save money compared to eating out or buying pre-packaged meals.

- **Healthier Choices**: Having ready-to-eat healthy meals on hand makes it easier to stick to a nutritious diet and avoid unhealthy fast food or snacks.

By incorporating these tips into your routine, you can streamline your meal prep process and enjoy quick, easy, and nutritious meals throughout the week.

GLENN WALTON

ENCOURAGEMENT TO STAY HEALTHY

Embarking on a journey to maintain a healthy lifestyle through quick and nutritious lunches is a fantastic step towards overall well-being. Remember, consistency is key, and every small effort counts. Whether you're preparing a fresh salad, a hearty wrap, or a vibrant bowl, you're making choices that benefit your body and mind. Embrace the process, enjoy the flavors, and celebrate your commitment to health. Keep exploring new recipes, trying different ingredients, and finding joy in nourishing yourself. You've got this!

Additional Resources For Healthy Eating

- **Websites**:
    - **MyFitnessPal**: Offers a comprehensive database of recipes, nutritional information, and meal planning tools.
    - **EatingWell**: Provides healthy recipes, meal plans, and nutrition advice tailored to various dietary needs.
    - **Minimalist Baker**: Focuses on simple, quick recipes that require minimal ingredients and time, perfect for healthy eating.
- **Books**:
    - **"The Whole30: The 30-Day Guide to Total Health and Food Freedom" by Melissa Hartwig Urban**: A detailed guide to a transformative eating plan that emphasizes whole, unprocessed foods.

- **"How Not to Die: Discover the Foods Scientifically Proven to Prevent and Reverse Disease" by Michael Greger, M.D.**: Explores the impact of diet on health and provides practical advice for incorporating nutrient-rich foods into your diet.
- **"The Blue Zones Kitchen: 100 Recipes to Live to 100" by Dan Buettner**: Features recipes inspired by the diets of the world's longest-lived people.

- **Apps:**
  - **Yummly**: Offers personalized recipe recommendations based on your dietary preferences and restrictions.
  - **Mealime**: Provides meal plans and recipes designed to make healthy eating simple and enjoyable.
  - **Paprika Recipe Manager**: Helps you organize your recipes, create meal plans, and generate grocery lists.

By utilizing these resources, you can continue to expand your culinary skills, discover new and exciting recipes, and maintain a balanced, healthy diet. Happy cooking and enjoy your journey to better health!

THANK YOU

Thank you for joining us on this journey towards healthier eating. We hope you found the recipes and tips in this book both inspiring and practical. **If you enjoyed this book, please consider leaving a review.** *Your feedback not only helps us improve but also assists others in discovering and benefiting from this book.* **Happy cooking and stay healthy!**

Printed in Great Britain
by Amazon